Druk's Path

A Journey on the Back of a Dragon

by

To Rob & Ann-Shirley,
Enjoy the
Adventure !
Cheers —
Beverly

Beverly Lynne Gray

Sonnenschein Books
Black Forest Press
San Diego, California
May, 2003
First Edition, First Printing

Drukgyel Dzong, ruins of the ancient fort, shadowed by
Jhomolhari and the Bhutanese Himalayas
Location: Paro Valley, Bhutan

Druk's Path

A Journey on the Back of a Dragon

by

Beverly Lynne Gray

Printed in the United States of America
by
Black Forest Press
P.O. Box 6342
Chula Vista, California 91909-6342
(800) 451-9404 Contracts Administration and Inquiries
(888) 808-5440 Marketing, Sales and Promotion

Disclaimer

Cover design by Aurora Zhivago.

On the cover:

The cover depicts Drukgyel Dzong, built in 1649 to control the major trade route to Tibet. Destroyed by fire and left to ruin since 1951, its name - *Druk (Bhutan) Gyel (Victory)* celebrates the victory of Bhutan over Tibet in 1644.

Printed in the United States of America
Library of Congress
Cataloging-in-Publication
ISBN: 1-58275-084-X
Copyright May, 2003 by Beverly L. Gray

Himalayan Monal feathers

Some of the wildflowers of Bhutan

Acknowledgments

No work of art, especially writing, is ever done alone. There are many who make it happen, by giving of their time, their talent, their energy, or by just giving you space to create. I have a list of special people who were instrumental in making this book a reality, and collectively, are really the talents behind the tale. Thank you, each of you, for your time, your talent, your energy and for the space in my life that you fill which makes it whole.

To Dennis Sumwalt, who is my biggest fan and gives me both space to create and a wide berth for my wild spirit, who also contributed great photos and is the world's most congenial traveling companion.

To Brian Sumwalt, who created the sketches and art in the book from my descriptions, photos and sketches, feathers and flowers in my original journal, and who contributed both his talent for drawing and the sensitivity of a fellow author.

To Amy and Aaron Rhoades, who took responsibility for things at home while this tale took place—which made that worry one of those things I *didn't* have to think about.

To Penny Allen, who found Bhutan, the Land of the Thunder Dragon in the first place, and contributed her skills including much of the photography, early editing, and unrelenting encouragement.

To Jeanne Kearley, who added her talents to the editing process, and while reading my journal aloud to a group of women adventurers, gave it life early in the evolution of the journal becoming a book.

To Kinley, Belden, and Wongdi, who guided and guarded me along Druk's Path. Their skills as mountaineers and knowledge of their homeland are unsurpassed, and their cheerful smiles and quiet cordiality will always be remembered.

PHOTOGRAPHY: Courtesy of Penny Allen, Dennis Sumwalt, Beverly Sumwalt

ARTWORK: Courtesy of Brian Paul Sumwalt

MAP OF BHUTAN: Courtesy of Bhutan Travel

AUTHOR'S SKETCH PORTRAIT: Courtesy of Don Bennett

AUTHOR'S PHOTPGRAPHIC PORTRAIT: Courtesy of Mike Armbrust, Chula Vista Photo

Other books by Beverly Lynne Gray:

Thunderstorms and Rainbows

Dedication

This book is dedicated to
the woman who swam
with hippos at seventy-eight—

—and to wild spirits everywhere,
and the Dragons who guard and protect them.

Guardian Dragon
Artist: Unknown Bhutanese metal sculptor

Druk's Path
A Journey on the Back of the Dragon

When does an adventure actually begin? Is it at conception, as a thought still swirly with mists and undefined edges, with little form or function? Is it when you finally speak of it to friends and family and actually have an idea you can articulate? Is it at the planning stage when you set dates, buy gear and make lists? Or at the actual beginning, the catch in your breath at the sight of mountains or the chill in the wind as you pack your bags, or with the good-byes and good wishes as you leave your familiar comforts? My friends and I agree that a third of an adventure is in the talking and planning, a third in the doing, and a third in the story-telling after. With that thought, this adventure began years ago—and perhaps in some mysterious way this last third will be the most fun of all.

Himalayan mists surround The Tiger's Nest
Location: above Paro Valley, Bhutan

Prologue

Years ago, as a full-grown (but not necessarily grown up) adult, I began collecting dragons. Fierce ones, benevolent ones, famous ones, unique ones—dragons made of different materials and from different places, and with different stories and origins. Long before they were part of the now-popular culture in recent movies and video/computer games, dragons were secretive and harder to find. JRR Tolkein's *SMAUG* and *CRYSOPHYLLAX* are two of my favorites and both have icons resting in a state of casual observance from a shelf in my family room. I've found dragons in most every country where I have traveled, and each part of the world has its own brand of "dragon lore". Friends and family spot them for me and send them to me from all over, and there hasn't been a Christmas in decades that I have not received at least one as a gift. And of course, author Anne McCaffrey has made my world of dragons even more rich than my fertile but sometimes distracted mind could imagine.

A Bhutanese Dragon

With that history as a backdrop, you will understand the spark of interest that was generated when I heard somewhere about a trail in the Himalayas called "The Dragon's Back Ridge". I can't recall where I heard it or from whom, or if perchance I only dreamed about it—so I've chosen to believe it was a whisper in the ear from a little pewter dragon earring, sharing daydreams with me. At any rate, I kept it on the back burner and told myself that it was "on my list" and one of these days I'd find out where it was and take the hike. I'm not sure, but I believe THAT was the beginning of the adventure.

Years later, my good friend called me and said, "We have to take our next trip together to Bhutan. It's one of the world's loveliest places, and we should see it before the world changes it." "Besides," she said, "You'll love it, they call it *The Land of the Thunder Dragon*". Well, enough said, and I started reading.

Lo and behold, there it was, right in the western part of the country in the foothills of the Bhutanese Himalayas—*Druk's Path*, ("*druk*" being the Bhutanese name for "dragon"). And to make it all the more symbolic I was approaching the infamous half-century mark and decided the journey was something I should do right after turning 50 years old. Needless to say I started making plans, and the first third of the adventure was well under way.

"If I'm going to be that close…"

Anyone who has planned an international trip knows how complicated it can be. I prefer to travel on my own agenda, and structure things outside of what the travel industry calls "packages". Working with an experienced travel agent makes it easier, but in this case there were too many variables and my companions and I had to do most of the planning ourselves.

The trip began to take shape and my *mantra* became, "if we're going to be that close, I need to see…" which made things interesting. The upshot of all this ended up becoming several side excursions before reaching Bhutan—and in retrospect, certainly laid the groundwork and mental preparation for the journal I had planned to write while hiking on the back of my mountain Dragon. So, "if I'm going to be that close, I need to tell you about…"

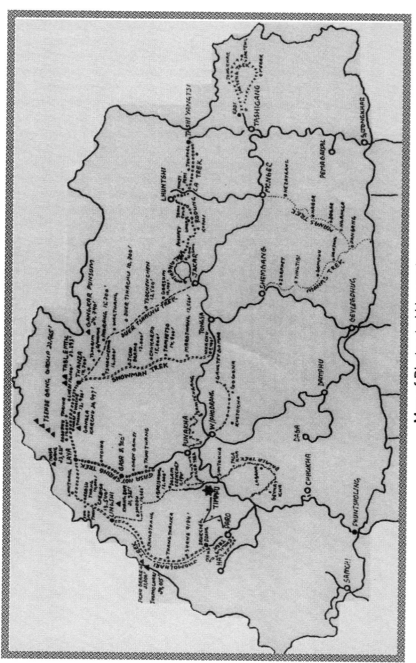

Map of Bhutan trekking routes

India

Buffalo cart and driver taking hay to market
Location: countryside near Agra, India

Leaving Western civilization in the jet trail, we arrived in New Delhi via Bangkok, and with little sleep. Our luggage was left at LAX. Therein lies one of the great mysteries of travel—and unfortunately, one that will not be solved in my lifetime. Without makeup, personal items, clean undergarments, (much less clothes or even spare shoes), we arrived at an old and elegant hotel, an obvious remnant of the British Raj. It was easy to see I would be a little under-dressed for dinner. It was evening there; we were exhausted, but ventured out for a quick shopping trip to buy a few essentials. Walking one block from the hotel found me at a street market, much like our drive-in parking lot swap meets. I bought socks, sleepwear, a couple tee shirts, and undergarments. Indian women are not built like western women—and "fit" is obviously not part of "design". After four days and much ado, our luggage finally caught up to us. But for several days I was attired in exactly the same and rather unflattering outfit.

The reason for the India side trip was to see the Taj Mahal. The train to Agra left before dawn and the bustle of a morning train station gave me the feeling of being a stranger in a strange land. Signs were in Hindi and Sanskrit and the train ticket was the only secret to boarding the right train car. The smells of bodies and diesel smoke mixed to cause a sickening sweet smell that was difficult to cope with before a steaming cup of coffee. The train left the station, and the light of first dawn ushered pictures through the windows fogged with breath and humidity. Shapes began to take on the form of people and shanties and cattle, blurring slightly as the train picked up speed. The rattle and rhythm of the train car took us out of New Delhi and we headed south amid what was hopelessly abject poverty along the train route. Not unexpected, but unsettling just the same. People accustomed to being watched as a train rattles by begin their morning in much the same way as people have for centuries, before there were trains and tracks to be used as latrine facilities. I cope with the sudden vision of monsoon rains washing down the train track hills into the gutters and animal pens, onto the dirt floors of the houses and through the back doorways to the family garden—it is graphically clear that the pain and disease and death associated with overpopulation is directly proportional to the quality of sanitation and hygiene. My bottled water held tightly in my hands becomes more precious with each mile as the sun rises on the generations of India with the sameness of infinity.

Agra is a city of tourism, with histories and stories unlike anywhere I've ever been— and the Taj Mahal is breathtaking, awesome, beyond belief.

Sunrise over the
Taj Mahal
Location:
Agra, India

I was moved by it for different reasons and came away with conflicted feelings about its beauty and history. Its majesty and mystery helped to set the tone for the rest of my journey. Walking silently inside the cool, semi-darkness of the unbelievably ornate monument to this young woman gave me an eerie sense of the fragility of life, the meaning and the meaninglessness of it all, and the sadness and joy we all experience. On the brink of a very small adventure in a very big world, my heart went out to the young woman who was captured for all eternity in a dark-white sarcophagus of cold marble and may or may not have ever had her dreams fulfilled. In so many ways, I have had so many more choices, and I was deeply moved by that thought.

The drive back to New Delhi was an adventure all by itself. Trucks with *"Tata OK"* which means "Please Honk" on the back, brahma cattle casually lying in the middle of four-lane traffic, camels and buffaloes decorated with ribbons and racing stripes hauling carts of grain were all part of the scene.

Everything's welcome on the streets of India
Location:
South of
New Delhi, India

"Racing camel" and drivers with a load of grain for market
Location:
Outside of
Agra, India

If you could just "go with the flow" you were OK. No one who has ever driven a California freeway would survive over there behind a wheel—but the odd thing was, there was absolutely no "road rage". People just moved in, out, around, honked, waved, (not gestured, mind you). I imagine it like watching a two-step in a country bar from the ceiling—no one actually ever runs into each other although from the ground it appears to be chaos. Due to a milk truck which had overturned up ahead, (no one was crying, however, they were all joking and laughing even though they were stuck in traffic) our driver took a u-turn right in the middle of the highway, drove in and out through the cars lined up on the opposite side like they were pylons for a road race, and took us on a detour through a smallish city off to the east. It was something to see.

The car was the only motorized vehicle on the dirt road, amid camels, buffaloes, carts, bicycles, and mostly people. People were on every square inch of the landscape: sitting, standing, riding, crowding, cooking, eating, talking, selling, buying, arguing, begging, and taking care of personal business in the street gutters. But they all had one thing in common—they were all looking at us. It was obvious that westerners, especially blond or auburn haired women, in a car no less, were not your everyday experience. People brought their children to the sidewalk and pointed. Old men held their beads to our car windows.

"Local color" beads for sale
Location: small town north of Agra, India

I was awestruck, and in shock as the total population density of this small town slowly rose to my conscious mind and the reality of our different lifestyles set in. As this all unfolded, our driver calmly just kept driving, using his horn, moving amidst the throng of bodies and no one got hurt or angry. After about an hour we were back on the highway again moving toward the severely over-populated and multi-stratified layer of life in New Delhi. Little was said—there was little we could say.

The Rumdoodle - Kathmandu's famous Climber's Bar
Location: the Thamel District, Kathmandu, Nepal

Nepal—Kathmandu

The next little side trip, casually but craftily orchestrated as a result of my *mantra*, was Kathmandu and the Royal Chitwan National Park. Ever since the scene in the mountain bar in *Raiders of the Lost Ark*, I've always wanted to drink whiskey in a sherpa bar in Kathmandu. It seemed exotic, wild, a little (well, maybe a lot) on the edge—my kind of thing. So as you might imagine, "if I'm going to get that close...." I drank whiskey in the most famous climbers' bar in the city called The Rumdoodle, right in the heart of Thamel, the "night life" district. It certainly wasn't as wild and wooly as the movie version, and most of the clientele had showered recently. But it was obvious from the wall graffiti that it was THE quintessential *before-and-after-the-ascent climbers' bar*. That was good enough for me.

With whiskey in hand, I shared a story that I had forgotten for years with my fellow bar-mates. I was once the only woman student on a field research trip with a group of biology graduate students, and each night at campfire we drank beer and tried to out-do each other with inventing outlandish research projects. The existence of the Abominable Snowman (The Yeti, or Sasquatch) became a favorite topic and it was decided that in order to capture a living one to prove the validity and viability of the species, it would be necessary to stake out a female, preferably one in full estrous cycle—as a decoy. Being the only female in the group, it was natural that I should volunteer. (Actually, in retrospect, I think I *was* volunteered!) After all, I was "just one of the guys", you know, and all that. Under the influence of everyone's favorite brew, we elaborated, we challenged each other, we planned out the whole capture and anyone listening would have thought the group was absolutely serious—and absolutely nuts. I never forgot the high-energy tongue-in-cheek humor over that plot, and secretly thought it might just work if the creature really existed. Then, in my reading about Bhutan, I discovered they believe the Yeti *does* exist and have even designated land in Eastern Bhutan to preserve its habitat and breeding grounds. When I told my companions this we all had a round of toasts to the possibilities of my becoming "Yeti Bait" and the rest of our conversation grew suitably improper enough for a Kathmandu sherpa bar.

Kathmandu is a remarkable place, with clashes of Eastern, Western, religion, dress, art and cuisine that all seem to melt together in harmony. It is cosmopolitan and yet ancient, bustling and yet serene, diverse and yet unified. The closest comparison might be Hong Kong, but even that is a stretch. I walked through some of the oldest and the newest of the tri-cities that make up Kathmandu, and stayed right down the street from the palace where, a mere three weeks after our visit the Crown Prince assassinated the Royal Family members. It was tragic, and seemed so personal having just been there, seeing and hearing much about the Royal Family. Our city escapades took us to the ancient city of Bhaktapur where no vehicles are allowed and the entire economy consists of barter. Clay pottery is a major item, chickens are tied to a brick with string around their foot in the front yard-patch, and girls wash their hair in a bucket alongside a riverbed cluttered with hogs sleeping in the warm mud of the noonday sunshine. Old men played "Goat and Tiger" with rocks and sticks on the street corners, betting on the outcome and grinning toothlessly and inviting us to place our bets. A group of young boys played ping-pong in the shade of a pottery kiln. Their paddles were fashioned out of asymmetrical pieces of plywood with a handle, and the net was an ankle- high makeshift wall of bricks. They had drawn the lines in hard-packed dirt and had a real ping pong ball and invited me to take a turn, then laughed as I "bombed out" and sent me to the back of the line. The language of children is universal—and words are unimportant when there is laughter to be shared. We adults have forgotten how to communicate with play.

The local economy of Bhaktapur
Location: Bhaktapur in Kathmandu, Nepal

Young girl
washing her hair
Location:
Bhaktapur,
Kathmandu, Nepal

Old men playing the street game "Goat and Tiger"
Location: Bhaktapur, Kathmandu, Nepal

Young boys play ping-pong in the village square
Location: Bhaktapur, Kathmandu, Nepal

Unique among experiences on this trip was sunrise over the Himalayas. Dhulikhel is a town about a two-hour drive into the foothills where one can see the entire Himalayan range at the crossroads to Tibet. The visible range includes such wonderful exotic names of peaks as Langtang-Lirung, Melungtse, Dorje-Lakpa and Karylung. Each peak has multiple names—the ones given by eastern lore, the ones given by their own countries, and the ones given by western climbers. It's impossible to master the pronunciation, and we know the most famous ones by their western names. We stay at the local resort (and I use the term loosely) where the rooms had floor to ceiling windows overlooking the mountain range to the north. Rising very early, I joined the few hearty souls who went to the top of the lodge to watch the sunrise—a spiritual moment to be sure. My traveling companions are all photographically experienced and I can barely remember to take the camera, so I was standing off by myself trying very hard to avoid listening to the discussions on F-stops and exposures for the perfect sunrise shot. Moving into a space of meditation and awe as I watched that spot on the horizon where the sun would peek over the most majestic mountains in the world, I felt my pulse begin to quicken in anticipation. I wanted to actually see the first rays, the splay of color, and the rim of the white-hot light that begins the day at the top of the world. I'd been blocking out the background conversations when one of my companions came up to stand behind me saying, "Look over there!" and pointed to my left. Out of courtesy I looked, rather than say "shhh" or "leave me alone please" — and in so doing, missed that moment in time and space that my soul had waited patiently to see. Covering my disappointment was one of the hardest things I've ever had to do—and there is part of me still chaffing. There are moments in time one can never repeat, and that was one of them. Lesson learned: look carefully, speak softly, and tread lightly for it is unforgivable to interrupt someone's spiritual moment.

Later that morning, admittedly in a less than buoyant mood I hiked with the group up a hot, dusty and difficult trail to a small Hindu temple that claimed the best views of the peaks. Being first, (the photographers were at work) I walked up three ancient stone steps to the tiny temple courtyard and came literally face to face with the recently attached head of a goat. We had stumbled onto a blood sacrifice ceremony to the Goddess Kali being carried out by a small family—an ancient crone grandmother, a young woman and her three or four year old son and two young men, one perhaps the father, the other an uncle. It was both moving and disconcerting at the same time and like nothing I had ever seen. The goat had been sacrificed, the family was performing the ceremonies that had gone on here from time before time, and we were totally and cor-

Blood sacrifice to the Goddess Kali, a spring and fall ritual
Location: Temple outside Dhulikhel, Nepal

dially ignored. If it had been possible they would have walked right through us instead of past us as we watched and were nonplussed by our presence or our cameras. I was still sulking from my "less than peak" experience at sunrise, and felt we had all intruded on something they considered sacred, feeling uncomfortable and like we had "interrupted a spiritual moment". But in reality, as I replay it in my mind, they seemed to be able to capture a space that I could not—able to have their moment uninterrupted by the outside world and to stay in their own space. My space, on the other hand, is easily disturbed and no doubt a product of western social consciousness and/or sensory overload. The art of "tuning the world out" belongs to the eastern religions. Perhaps personal space and spirituality are products of *cultivation* and not *civilization*. Truly a concept for future exploration—yet I will always see the bloody head of a black and white goat as an icon of that disconnectedness. Having voiced my displeasure to my companions for what to me appeared to be an intrusion, I then had to also apologize for my own disconnectedness.

Royal Chitwan National Park

There is something about a tiger. Aside from tragically being eastern cultural aphrodisiacs and western world fur coats, they inspire our imagination. Who among us has not seen these magnificent creatures in the local zoo? And if lucky enough to meet their gaze, who has not been captured by the beauty, the power, the intelligence, the warning and wonder that emanates from the eyes of this majestic cat? There is much that civilization has created and much it has destroyed—and the habitat of some of the worlds' most beguiling creatures is one of them. Armed with the knowledge that they are already a compromised breeding species, we took off to the Terai Arc region of Nepal where there are still tigers living wild.

I was obsessed with seeing one and most anxious to be on our way. Then I saw the airplane. Yeti Airlines (seriously!!) handed me a boarding card with the picture of a tiger on it, and gestured for me to head for the plane which just barely met my criteria for flight capabilities. Flying never bothers me, but small planes with the cockpit visible from the last seat and earplugs as a necessity stretch my ability to "act casually". When the engines roared into submission and we began the ascent off the tarmac, you could not hear yourself think much less talk. I figured if I shouted no one would hear me anyway, so I'd better find some way to keep from peeling the leather off the arm rests. The pilots jockeyed us through canyons with the ease of familiarity, and I began to relax until I looked out the tiny window to my left only to see that the ridge tops were level with the wing tips—which meant we were zigzagging in

The Yeti Airlines
experience to
Tiger Tops
Location:
Tiger Tops
Air Terminal
Terai Arc Region,
Nepal

and around mountain ridges as if they were switchbacks and we were a car. Blanching for no one's notice, my mind reviewed how long it might take for a rescue yak to reach us and gave up on surviving if we "tipped" one of those ridges with a wing. My anxious mind began working overtime and created a new medical transport company—"Yak-Evak"—leaving me to wonder if you could actually ride one of those things.

Fortunately, good and experienced pilots are to be cherished and we arrived without incident as my rational mind knew we would. Ten minutes out they radioed to have the runway cleared of cattle so we could land on a grass runway bordering a small thatch-roofed village. Children ran alongside the runway, waving and shouting at the plane. We were invited into the terminal for a cool drink and to meet our guides for the trip into the jungle. Gathering my gear, I moved out and down the rickety ladder steps. The air smelled of fuel, hot tires and dry grass, and the hazy light was blinding. It was stiflingly hot and humid as I walked slowly away from the plane, unable to take my gaze off the dazzling starkness and simplicity of this place. The terminal was an open-air thatched patio with canned drinks and imported ice, obviously a luxury stashed on the plane for tourists. My first thought was "this definitely isn't Kansas anymore" as we shook hands with people, accepted cordial hospitality, and pointed out bags for porters who were anxious to be off.

It's hard to describe the feelings that cascade through your mind as your senses become overwhelmed in an attempt to take it all in—the vegetation, the smells, the casual chat in foreign tongues, the dust in your clothes as the jeeps move over dirt roads and dodge tree branches and rocks. You have to catalog them, file them, and take them out for review later or you loose the magic of it all, so I was processing as rapidly as my brain would allow. And, every forth or fifth thought was "I'm actually going to see tigers!" My eyes were keen, looking at as much as I could possibly take in, hoping that one might even lunge across our path as we traveled toward the jungle lodge that would be our quarters for the next three days. In retrospect I could have napped. No self-respecting tiger would be caught dead anywhere near all that ruckus of two jeeps and seven adults. But hey, I was up for the adventure, and hoping for the best. We came to the banks of a smallish river, got out of the jeep, crossed the river in a dugout canoe, got into another jeep sent to meet us, and traveled on in the dust and heat. We did that three times, and then shouldered our backpacks (porters had taken our sparse but heavy gear bags on footpaths—no jungle jeeps for them!) and we hiked the last 30 minutes on foot crossing sandy streambeds through tall stands of lowland forested areas and semi-jungle-like landscape. Sweating, swatting the occasional fly, and tripping about every 30 feet because I kept looking around instead of watching my steps, my obsession grew. This was like nothing I'd ever done, like no place I'd ever been. I just had to see a tiger.

At the end of the trail, I walked right into the most luxurious tent camp I'd ever seen. There was a large veranda, full bar, outdoor grill and huge deck surrounded by trees and overlooking a couple of Asian white rhinos just having an afternoon snack in the cleared area off the deck. Cameras flashed, we all relaxed and enjoyed the palm-frond breezes of the fans above and the shade of the trees beyond. Our hosts treated us to delicacies, drinks, tidbits of history and descriptions of the area, and we were invited to "freshen up" as our first jungle jaunt to see the wildlife in the reserve was in about an hour. We were escorted to our tents down dirt trails lined with rocks and obviously swept free of leaves and debris most regularly. There were six tents and each was equipped with two twin beds, a small bench, an outdoor "water closet" with sink, shower and toilet all fed from sun-warmed water bags on the roof.

Tent Camp at Tiger Tops
Location: Royal Chitwan National Park, Nepal

We were cautioned to zip all the closures tightly each time we went in/out, as there were "creatures" who preferred the luxury of the tent to the wild outdoors, and not to be surprised to perhaps see largish spiders, snakes, and even monkeys hanging about. Well, I can deal with the snakes and the monkeys—but those "largish spiders" require drastic measures. I took a moment to just stand on the porch of the tent, looking out through very tall trees where a few small langurs cavorted in the branches and just listened to the sounds of a world unknown—so foreign, so exotic, yet so familiar. I felt strangely at home as if I'd been there before, as if I'd lived this moment of quiet noise that city-dwellers don't recognize, as if a part of me belonged in a place like this. Sometimes I wonder why my life took the paths it did, for clearly part of me was meant to be among the animals in wild places.

Contemplating the wildness of things, I joined the group and we embarked on a "first"—a ride on the back of an elephant into the riverine landscape of this reserve. Now, elephants are not particularly comfortable to ride, mind you, and even less so when you're "side-saddle". They put a large rack on the back of the beast, and then you sit on one side or the other, with the elephant's keeper in front on the neck and a second keeper standing with bare feet on the leathery hide just above the tail, holding on to the back rail of the "saddle" rack. Being large and graviportal, they rock from side-forward to side-forward and plant those man-crushing feet with purpose. It feels rather cushy and comfortable for about six steps. After that, it's a matter of positioning yourself to accept the least amount of

On elephant safari, in search of tigers
Location: Royal Chitwan
National Park, Nepal

bruise damage to your back, ribs, elbows, and rear-end bones as they bang against the wooden rack. Extra fat helps, but causes no long-lasting immunity. If the wildlife is on your side of the elephant, it's pretty cool. If it's on the other side, you can wrench your neck trying to turn a 180 with only your upper torso. But what fun, what an adventure, what a show! We saw rhinos, we saw bushbuck, we saw deer, we saw gaur, we saw monkeys, we saw waterfowl, we saw warthogs. We saw no tigers.

The haze of humidity collided with the dust and cooling air as dusk began to sneak over the landscape, and the sunset took on colors that cannot be recreated by anything human. The elephant carried us back to the veranda platform and condescendingly stood still, pumping elephant grass into his mouth while we laboriously and rather unceremoniously disembarked. I for one tried hard not to look too geriatric in my attempt to unfold limbs and climb off the saddle. Dinner, a culinary repast worthy of the best reviews, was accompanied by rousing conversation and recall of the day. By this time there were others there, a couple with two young girls. We introduced ourselves, ate and talked, and exchanged the usual polite amenities. I participated but was not really there—I watched those two girls, bored with the adults and without any real appreciation of where they were in the world, how wonderful and exotic this place was, how much they would miss of this experience since they were so young and self-absorbed. It struck me how much of life gets by us while we grow up, how little we "see" of the world. What would it be like if, from the moment we are born we embraced these experiences with the same awe and appreciation as we do in mid-life? Youth is presumptuous—and I think we miss too much getting to 25. Slowly and painfully rejoining conversation I am saddened to think this might be the only lifetime we get and wishing I could have a few more. So much to experience, so little time.

Sunset over the river
Location:
Tiger Tops Tent Camp
Royal Chitwan National Park, Nepal

Nothing like a "largish spider" to bring you right smack back to reality! The kerosene lamp used to illuminate the water closet cast imposing shadows as I made my way through the motions of preparing for bed. Had I seen the spider before I used the toilet, the night would have been completely unpleasant. Fortunately for me, I noticed him afterwards. He (or she, who cares) crawled out from under the seat and up the back to rest on the wall behind the toilet tank, casting a shadow the size of China on the wall behind. I remain proud of the fact that I did not screech, but kept my eye on the beast and cut my routine short. And, heeding the casual warning of our porter, I scanned the entire tent by flashlight and made certain zippers were tightly closed. I'm a quick learner.

This arachnoid experience, however, has one small thing to recommend it. It kept me awake. My angst over being crawled on certainly heightened my senses and I listened to the captivating and strange night sounds. It was difficult to discern between the quiet noise of flora and fauna or tents creaking, or soft wind sounds, yet I found myself guessing and no doubt would have been completely aghast at my errors. The night seemed both long and short, and before I knew it the pre-dawn light began to stir the world and seep into the dark spaces. With movements I hoped were stealthy, as I wanted solitude, I dressed and left the tent—grimacing at the noise the zippers made. One can make so much noise trying to be quiet! Every footfall on my short walk to the veranda seemed to echo into the jungle and I was certain I had alerted the whole camp of my upright mobility. I soon discovered that I was not the "earliest riser", there was already coffee made and quiet kitchen sounds coming from the outdoor cook stove where our cook was preparing for the morning meal. He smiled a huge, shy smile at me and nodded his head, knowing in some international way that I'd be headed for the coffee and pointed me in the direction of that universal morning habit with his eyes. I've become a social coffee drinker over the past few years, and somehow nothing seemed more "right" than a steaming cup held in both hands, as I positioned myself as far from people as possible to watch the day unfold.

We had been told not to leave the compound without a guide, and it was not said casually. A native naturalist appeared out of the veranda with his own cup in hand, to join me as I watched the mists climb skyward where the rhinos had been yesterday afternoon. He greeted me cheerfully yet in a whisper—respect for silence and quiet is a code of conduct when you work and live in wild places—and asked if I'd like to take a walk and look for early morning wildlife. He must have been reading my mind. He offered me a walking stick and we started off east down the trails and along the riverbed. Signs of rhinos who had trudged through the brush, wild pigs who'd been digging for grubs, and nesting beds of various dear and antelope were everywhere, and none too far from our camp. I began comparing noise notes with things he was pointing out, but they didn't seem to match and the mysteries remain unsolved. My cheerful guide walked briskly, but never failed to point or stop or show me signs of the jungle. I could not understand him and missed his names and explanations completely. Listening to heavily accented English in this part of the world needs an experienced ear, which I hadn't yet developed. But nonetheless, I managed to ask about tigers and he managed to tell me yes, occasionally he had seen one, but they were elusive. As we stood high in an animal blind used to observe the wildlife, he told me that a week ago a village woman came too far into the reserve to cut grass for her hut roof and had been killed and eaten by a tiger. A week ago. I asked him that again, and he said yes, just last week. This is definitely not Kansas. Once again impressed, I was startled out of that reverie by something very large moving through the underbrush near our platform with little concern for following footpaths. My guide whispered, "stand still, be very quiet" which he needn't have said it seemed so obvious. Then just to our left came a rhino female with her smallish baby, tossing her head and snorting, digging around in the brush and walking right under the blind and past us into the forest. Now a rhino is pretty impressive from afar, but causes a stir of unease when only about six feet from you and capable of knocking down the telephone poles of your "safe-place" just by bumping into them. Rooted to the floorboards, there wasn't even time for photographing the behemoth up close and personal. But the picture of their tails twitching casually as they disappeared into the brush will forever be in my memory banks. The jungle forest absorbed them back into its silence, and one by one the birds returned to their harmonious cacophony.

Back at the camp things were bustling by now, the sun having been up for nearly half an hour. Freshly brewed coffee and breakfast smells were abundant as we sat waiting for our elephant friend to take us out again. Shifting our seating arrangements didn't help the bruised places, but the morning wildlife made up for it.

Rhinoceros grazing in the early morning marshes
Location: Royal Chitwan National Park, Nepal

Every species was out and frisky, and we saw a repeat list of our previous safari through the river and brush. By now we'd seen enough rhinos that pictures weren't an event, so mostly we all just watched—and scanned the scene for that speck of orange and black, hoping it would be there.

It amazed me how quickly the day got muggy and hot, how the insects seemed to hone in on our sweaty necks and how the mist became heat waves in just one short elephant ride. Unfolding out of the wooden pachyderm saddle, we sauntered to our tents, packed up our gear and sent it off with porters to the Tiger Tops Lodge where we would spend our next night. They would travel with it on foot and wrapped it in a cargo net tied on a large bamboo pole suspended between them on their shoulders. We would travel by foot at a much more leisurely pace after we breakfasted.

The walk to the lodge was most pleasant, and cold drinks awaited us there. We'd been quietly alone at the tent camp, but this place was bustling with people—tourists, naturalists, students, lodge and restaurant attendants (who were also mostly students on biology internships) and even reporters. Our rooms were lovely, large, and cooled by jungle breezes through screened windows and the tepid shower quite the antidote for jungle heat. One of the naturalists gave an elephant lecture in the heat of the afternoon and then invited anyone interested to help give the elephants their daily bath in the river. An opportunity not to be passed up, I trudged the trail to the river with several other brave souls and plunged in to help rub and scrub one of the young ones. Elephants enjoy this time with people, and there was much splashing and water spurting. The elephant keepers shouted commands, checked feet and ears and trunks, and moved around their elephant with authority and some concern for safety. It would be easy for someone to be hurt, and in our country this would never have been allowed—the potential for lawsuit would be just too tempting.

Baby elephant gets a bath in the river Location: Royal Chitwan National Park, Nepal

After the elephants were clean and the people were dirty, we all headed back to our rooms and our naturalist talked to me for a while as we walked back to the lodge. I learned things about elephants that I hadn't known before, and he pointed out the large male "tusker" that we would ride next morning. This charming Nepalese man has a Masters' degree in biology, and had been working with the reserve for 19 years training and teaching many a park keeper and student intern the virtues and the balances of this fragile environment. The elephant lore alone made him a man of great fame and renown.

The elephant compound run by the Park naturalists and handlers Location: Royal Chitwan National Park, Nepal

Dinner, evening drinks, introductions to the key people at Tiger Tops and interesting conversation with other lodge guests gave the evening a festive atmosphere. Talk buzzed about two young students who just happened to be sitting in a blind overlooking the river just down the road from the main lodge. While they were sitting there, a tiger ran into the clearing chasing a wild boar, which squealed and zigzagged and got away. Stunned, they couldn't even talk for several minutes, and then raced back to the lodge with the tale of the day. Since only about 20% of the people who visit the reserve ever see a tiger, let alone one hunting, this was quite a moment of good fortune—and my heart swelled with renewed hope for our early morning safari, and no doubt, our last chance to see this rare sight.

At the break of dawn I rose to ride one final safari. The mists rolled upward off the marsh riverbeds and instinctively everyone whispered, somehow knowing that respect for the beauty of the day's beginning was in order. Our elephant driver moved us all out smartly, and we could see three other elephants in sort of a triangle, following the bed of the river. All at once, shouting started, much commotion arose, and you could hear the three drivers giving orders to their beasts—one of them had seen a tiger, and they were all moving toward it to flush it out. It felt like a "hunt", and the same excitement emanated from man and beast alike as we moved in circles, and just then the tiger made her move. She sprinted across the riverbed, stretching her body to full stride with paws reaching forward to dig into the earth and tail extended behind for

The elusive Tiger

balance. The grace and speed were magnificent, and my heart skipped a beat at the sight. No one managed to get a camera in hand, such was the beauty of the moment. Tears collected in my eyes, as I watched her disappear into the elephant grasses at the edge of the river, and as we followed and pushed her further, I saw her once more as her tail flicked in the air and hind feet jumped across a muddy space. And just as suddenly as she appeared, the tiger was gone. The quiet and mystique of the jungle seeped in behind her as if the space were never occupied by a tiger at all. I had seen a miracle—a wild, exotic, endangered and terribly beautiful miracle.

My visit to Chitwan totally complete in so many ways, we packed to leave and take the Yeti air-experience back to Kathmandu. While we waited for jeeps to assemble, the owner of Tiger Tops Lodge regaled us with stories and everyone was in high spirits. Holding "court", he was telling a story about the tusker we rode that morning. His keeper was in the hospital for surgery, and the "second man" was on vacation. Now elephants are quite particular about their keepers, and actually choose people rather than people choosing them. So, with the top two men out for a while, it fell to the "third man" to care for the elephant. Knowing it to be a promotion, he got a little cocky and haughty about "his elephant" and that this wasn't such a tough job caring for a tusker. The elephant took exception to that, and chose to use his tusks to pin him to the ground. Then, picking him up impaled on the tusks, he headed for the river 500 yards away, to the very place I had waded in waist deep only yesterday to bathe the elephants. The bull held the man underwater until he drowned, and then threw his body on the riverbank, charged back to the keeper's village and sought out his house among the row of grass-roofed shacks where keepers and their families lived. The tusker tore it apart, stomped it into the ground, without so much as touching a flower or rail on the houses to either side—and when he had made his social commentary quite clear about his feelings for this upstart keeper, he rampaged into the jungle trumpeting his anger and frustration to the world.

In the crisis, his keeper was summoned back by ambulance and arrived on a stretcher. The "second man" was called back from vacation and they were sent into the jungle to find and deal with the beast. They spent five days with him in the jungle, chained to a tree and medicated, calming him down and insisting they were back and would not leave him, and that it was time to return to the herd and the village and stop misbehaving. He regained his docile demeanor and they returned, and he has been working again without incident for the last six months. Six months. The impact of that hit me—that I had ridden an elephant that had killed a man, only *six months* ago. The world I live in is so protected, so un-dangerous by comparison. A man's life and home were destroyed, but the elephant went calmly back to work and six months later, brought me the miracle of a tiger. How marvelously strange the circle of life is when I stop long enough to feel it rotate around me.

BHUTAN

The Himalayas ranged to our left, snow capped and mysterious, the sky so blue your eyes hurt looking at it. The pilot introduces peaks to us with names familiar only from books about historic mountain climbs. He also gives us the native names that are unpronounceable to the unpracticed western tongue. Photographs are attempted through the double glass of airplane windows and people strain and climb over each other to see Mt. Everest at eye level. Snow is gusting off the tip of the mammoth mountain and one can almost feel the power of unsympathetic wind, ice and sun—Earth's reminder that she is a thing of beauty as well as treachery. As we fly past the endless majesty of these mountains I feel the intensity of knowing that in five days time I will be hiking among them, part of them, along the back of a Dragon who lives near the fifth highest peak in the range. A mixture of excitement and fear causes a shudder as I squint at the white-on-blue outside my airplane window.

Mt. Everest and the Himalayan Range
Location: Himalayan Range at 20,000 feet
along the Nepal/Tibet border

The runway into the Paro valley is narrow and stretches parallel to the river with little to spare in what this non-pilot prefers to call the "swerve factor": if you swerve, your wing tips hit the adjacent mountains. Twice while we were staying in the valley, the pilot missed and had to pull up, go around, and try it again. Fortune smiles, because that did not happened the day we landed or the leather armrests might have been destroyed at the vicinity of my seat assignment. As I got off the plane, it was as if I'd stepped into an ancient world. My feet were on a tarmac, but my eyes and mind were bombarded with the colors on the terminal building, voices in soft sounds of the Bhutanese language, the blue of the sky and the green of the hills that so recently had kissed the wings of the plane. Everything seemed foreign yet familiar in a way that I'm unable to describe and I knew that my adventure in this tiny, unknown country would be nothing if not unique.

Our guide, Chorten, found us and formally welcomed us to his country with white silk prayer shawls draped around our necks in the same way one receives a lei in Hawaii. They are given as gifts of respect and honor and used among the Bhutanese not just for tourists, but also for their own dignitaries, in their own temples, schools, and celebrations. Our time in Bhutan would not be our own and you are only allowed into the country on their terms which means a pre-paid visit, the accompaniment of a full time guide and

driver, and pre-arranged accommodations and meals. We were allowed "free time" for walking and some shopping but otherwise were accompanied. As it turned out, this was not oppressive— indeed it was done with the utmost courtesy and grace, and Chorten and our driver Samba were soon our good friends.

We drive through Paro, the second largest city in Bhutan on our way to lunch. The main street is unpaved with small shops and businesses along either side. You can walk its length in ten minutes with time to stop and look in shop windows. Most of the signage is in Dzongkha (the traditional and formal Bhutanese language) and some also in English albeit loosely

Colorful signs and translations along the streets and doorways
Location: Paro, Bhutan

translated. My favorite is a sign above a small restaurant and inn that says "Fooding and Lodg". Chorten tells me that English has been taught in their schools for many years and most everyone

Curious, happy and beautiful Bhutanese school children Location: Paro, Bhutan

under the age of 25 can speak English. The traditional Dzongkha is used for communication, and English reserved for international business and tourism. For a proud and traditional country of self-imposed isolation, Bhutan is also progressive and forward thinking. As it moves cautiously toward westernized ways and begins to enter the 20th century, the goal is not to diffuse any of the traditions and religious practices that hold the country united.

The Spring Festival, or "Tshechu" as it is called was one of the main reasons for visiting this country. Instructions were given since we were to attend the beginning dances that afternoon. The festival is five days of folk dances and folk songs and stories and booths selling local crafts and souvenirs and foods. It reminded me of a cross between the Passion Play and a County Fair, for lack of a better way to describe it. The Tshechu is a Buddhist ceremony that reviews the religious history of the region and prepares the people of the valley for the hanging of a

Festival marketplace - hearth brooms for sale Location: Paro, Bhutan

Festival marketplace - weighing produce
Location: Paro, Bhutan

Festival marketplace - skeining wool
Location: Paro, Bhutan

huge silk tapestry called the Thanka or Thongrol. Each day, many dances and songs are performed in a great open-air stone-paved courtyard and everyone who could walk the distance is there.

Paro Dzong, the site of the Spring Festival
Location: Paro, Bhutan

Looking out over the feast of colors in the crowd, I am reminded of the biblical story of the Feeding of the Five Thousand and wonder (not for the first or last time on this journey) at the similarities among the world religions which seem to be much more abundant than the differences between them.

To say I was fascinated by the costumes and the dances would be an understatement. While crammed in among bodies of women in their colorful *kiri* and men in their traditional *gho* and prayer shawls and children politely pushing to reach a spot where they can see, I am feeling very much like an outsider. There is no way to "blend" into the crowd. Even I am taller than most, and children look at me with curiosity while adults with beetle-nut stained teeth smile shyly and move in and out of the crowded scene with the universal rhythm that people at county fairs seem to have. Everywhere there was a feast for the eyes, the sounds of the temple horns and cymbals and bells were foreign and exotic and disturbingly discordant. Chants of ancient tales accompanied barefoot

dancers with green and yellow flared skirts and masks fixed with
tall antlers. We were watching the Dance of the Four Stags—a
leading dance of the Tshechu, and one could get lost in the monot-
ony of the movements and the singsong of the chants without much
difficulty.

Dance of the
Four Stags
at the
Spring
Festival
Location:
Paro, Bhutan

Our western culture is fraught with speed, with hurry-up
activity, with impatience and it has permeated our very essence.
For example, this celebration takes five days. One dance could be
described in a short paragraph, and yet takes hours to perform. We
have culturally evolved to need a shorter half-life for entertainment.
Our movies are under three hours, our plays have intermissions,
and even our children's books last only a few minutes if you read
slowly. But here, life is time and time is essence and essence is
being and being is life. The stories have been told for centuries, the
dances depicting the same scenes and costumes and moves over
and over, and yet people sit captivated by them. And much as I
wanted to absorb all of it, see each dance, taste and smell and feel
the heat and the crowd and the people, I suddenly knew that it could
not be that for me. All I could absorb was all I could absorb, and
the sensory overload took its toll by helping me to decide to miss a
dance and stroll the booths or join my friend for a walk through the
temple courtyard. Throughout the five days of the Spring Festival,
I experienced it in that way—until the early morning on the fifth
day.

The calendar date for Tshechu is set each year very much like we set the dates for Easter—based on the cycle of the full moon, and aligned with the Spring Equinox. The night is very clear and very cold, and the full moon lights our way as we walk up the hill to the monastery to find a place on the cold stair steps where we could view the processional of the monks carrying the sacred Thanka for hanging in the Dzong courtyard. Few speak, and what is said is in whispers. Many carry candles and incense or teapots of melted rancid butter for offering and there is some jockeying for position to view the procession. Tourists are told that photographs are appropriate, and the few foreigners sprinkled around among the locals are preparing camera equipment and checking batteries and flashes.

Gongs sound, chants begin, bells ring. The wooden monastery doors with large ring handles creak slowly open and the youngest monks in red novice robes emerge two by two from the gaping mouth in the whitewashed walls of Paro Dzong. They carry candles, and walk slowly past the well and up the stair steps where I am sitting close enough to smell the odors of young men whose bodies were recently washed but whose clothes were not. The procession continued with older acolytes, their teachers, the elder dancers, the women folk singers, the monk dancers, the priests and venerable lamas, and finally the Chief Abbot of Bhutan, the Je Khenpo and his attendants. Behind him, stripped to the waist and in white skirts and barefoot, come the Thondrol bearers—monks carrying the red silk-covered Thangka, rolled like a huge carpet and carried on their two rows of shoulders.

Sacred Thangka on the shoulders of the monks
Location: Paro Dzong, Paro, Bhutan

The ritual is powerful and mystical, and very similar to the trip to Golgotha with Jesus carrying the cross on his shoulders followed by the masses. It moves me once again how similar this is to our Easter story of resurrection and redemption. The Thondrol is unfurled briefly during Tshechu and is a tapestry depicting Guru Rimpoche and his eight manifestations. It is said it took 100 monks 100 years to create it, and the colors and size alone would certainly support that legend. It is believed that one's sins are washed away simply by viewing the tapestry, whose name literally means "the sight of which liberates". It is also believed that those who have a great desire to be delivered from transmigratory existence must protect this ancient custom and pass it on to future generations.

The Thangka has never been touched by the rays of the sun since it was made, and is hung with much chanting and singing before dawn. Young monks pull it from the bottom upwards until it covers the wall to the east of the great courtyard and the benevolent gaze of the Guru Rimpoche falls on the sacred dance floor and those who came to worship. It goes up slowly, allowing monks to set up worship altars, build huge incense fires and light butter candles. People begin to queue up, although there are no men in reflective vests with bullhorns directing people and no one organizing any formal order to the worship service. Everyone seems to know what to do, and the atmosphere is rather like the pleasant solemnity we find at sunrise services when they're held on some dew-covered hillside rather than in a church. Slowly and quietly people begin to sink into themselves, worshipping and accepting the grace of forgiveness in this holy place among their cultural and sacred rituals. Thousands pass by the Thangka, accepting its blessings, and people choose to add incense to the fires or butter to the butter candles. Some pray and kneel in meditation, reminiscent of worshipers saying rosary prayers, and are oblivious to those around them including the rude flashing of tourist cameras in their faces. In our culture such behavior would be quickly chastised, but here, the gift of inwardness allows for the blunders of thoughtlessness.

The sky perceptibly lightens as dawn approaches and the Holy Assembly of Monks begin the dances and services associated with the Thondrol unveiling. The mood turns more festive and I even spy a couple very young monks sitting cross-legged, yawning most unceremoniously. The mountain ridges to the east climb high above the monastery and the sun has to climb high before it makes its entrance above the valley of worshipers. Within a few hours, I

Sacred Thondrol unveiled on the wall of the Paro Temple at dawn
on the fifth day of the Spring Festival
Location: Paro Dzong, Paro, Bhutan

will be looking down on this site from high in those very mountains
on my ascent up the ridge to ride on the back of the Dragon. Tired
from the nearly all night vigil and shivering from the bone-chilling
cold of dawn, I am suddenly moved to tears with emotion. I am one
who has looked on the sacred Thangka, one whose transgressions
have been gifted with spiritual grace. My adventure into the mountains will be pure, spiritual and blessed. Pensively, I leave the Paro
Tshechu to begin a journey of the body but also of the soul.

And as the sun rises over the mountain ridge to the north-
east of Paro Valley announcing a new day, my Journey on the Back
of a Dragon begins. . .

Packing up with my trekking crew
Location: Trailhead, Druk's Path
Paro, Bhutan

THE JOURNEY

As written in my journal, beginning:

April 7, 2001

It is the evening before my trek—along the back of a Dragon called *Druk's Path* through the foothills of the Himalayas. And while it is no climb of Mt. Everest, this long awaited walk through the valleys and mountain passes will be no small task for me. I'm excited, I'm intimidated, I'm determined, I'm nervous. But what an adventure this will be.

Dinner with my friends (both American and Bhutanese), hearing jokes and encouragement, followed by a long and leisurely bath is a good way to begin. We will all attend the culmination of the Paro Spring Festival at dawn, the unfurling of the sacred Thangka (the Thondrol). This Buddhist blessing will send me off with a spiritual mindset and a circle of protection. In a world of such fast pace and where time is a commodity to be treasured, I'm very much looking forward to days of uninterrupted solitude. No parts to play, no masks to wear, no others to please. This is for me.

I will read *The Snow Leopard*. I will smell clean air and taste wind and weather. I will make dragons out of clouds and smile at every crow that follows me. I will light a candle and drink port every night, sending wishes to the heavens—I'll be so much closer, perhaps they'll come true. I will pick wildflowers every day and clear my wild and untamed mind of everything unimportant. I will walk the Dragon's Back and just perhaps catch a fleeting glimpse of who I really am.

April 8, 2001

The adventure begins. I met my guide and cook just below the Paro Museum where the trail begins. Kinley, a tall and capable-looking young man, is most pleasant and speaks perfect English. Belden, the cook, has a bright smile and seems easy going and ready to please. Several others mill around, packing horses and arranging equipment, and it seems to be overkill for just one lone hiker. I will be carefully and elaborately attended it appears.

Laughing and eager to be off, I say goodbyes to my traveling companions who wish me well, and watch as I head off uphill. I can see them as they wave one last time and climb in the white

View of the valley from the trail's first climb
Location: Above Paro Valley, Bhutan

van for their own adventure in the backcountry of Eastern Bhutan to places I will not see. I walk quietly for the next while, contemplating how I am now alone in the presence of people I don't know, heading for difficult mountain passes and uncertain weather, and challenged with physical demands I may not be able to meet. Overwhelmed with the sudden onset of "aloneness", I plod on wondering what ever possessed me to do this.

Later that morning:

We have hiked now nearly two hours, and all of it straight up. I am winded easily, and find I must stop nearly every one hundred yards or so. The altitude is no small thing with which to reckon. Kinley allows me to keep my own pace, and enters conversation with respect for my need to just walk and breathe and embrace the awe I always feel in the mountains. He and I will get along fine. The ponies have just passed me, and it is time to address this Dragon again.

The silence
of the wind
on moss, hangs
like veils on long
forgotten brides—
my senses sharpen
as blood pounds in
my ears and throbs
in swollen fingers—
a rhythm much faster
than my feet are
capable of moving.
The lack of synchrony
makes me edgy
for I tend to love
balance in all things—
even my own slow
and laborious pace.
I hear the wind as
it crawls through
the trees, enjoying
a sudden moment
with a crow, cawing
his approval in discord
somewhere overhead.

We hike steadily, slowly ever so slowly uphill. It seems and truly is, unrelenting. My sturdy young guide patiently keeps my pace, but I can tell he is used to much longer strides and smoother walking. It is hot, I've become reacquainted with sweat glands I forgot I had, and am glad of having both my hat and short-sleeved shirt.

We stop in a "yak meadow" for lunch of boiled eggs, boiled potatoes, a scrambled egg sandwich, apple and juice. Belden the cook has caught up to us by now and carried this cold and welcome repast in a pail. I was hungry. I don't think he speaks English, as Kinley addresses him in Dzongkha and then speaks for him. He smiles a lot, though, and will no doubt become my new best friend this afternoon when a cup of tea becomes priceless.

I turn to look through the tree branches to the valley below, the last I will see of Paro for several days, and see the magenta blooms of a plum tree and the roof of the last farmhouse high off the valley floor. The rocks placed on the roof to keep the boards from being torn off by the winds define the symmetry of life in a strange and yet familiar way as I turn to leave the last of the world behind.

Last view of the valley
Location:
Above
Paro Valley,
Bhutan

Rooftop - last farmhouse on the trail
Location:
Above Paro
Valley, Bhutan

Mid-afternoon:

The clouds came in, and the hike got serious. I've had to walk slowly and stop very frequently just to continue. Kinley keeps reassuring me that my pace is appropriate, and that the two other hikers we have seen are courting altitude sickness as they power by. I've decided not to offer apologies for myself and strive to enjoy the slow but steady pace I have set rather than be competitive.

We hike up—I go alone, knowing I'm followed but seeing no one. I find the startling purple and blue feathers of a male monal, one of Bhutan's beautiful birds. I hear eaglets complaining for dinner in a nest too well camouflaged to see, and hear the warning teeth

Himalayan Monal and feather

clicking of a wild boar whose shadowy outline is visible in the steep forest growth just above me. It is difficult to climb without stumbling, my legs are burning with the effort and I wonder if Kinley (who is keeping me in his sights no doubt) sees and worries that I might be showing signs of altitude sickness. He has already told me several stories of "the ones he had to carry down the mountain after dark". I'll disappoint him on that score, since I'm feeling excellent—if you minus out fatigue and lack of oxygen and lactic-acid-laced muscles.

Unexpectedly we reach the crest of this ridge, at 3450m (about 12,000 feet). All of a sudden, around one more endless bend in the trail I can see blue of the skyline and the outline of Jili Dzong, a 15th century monastery abandoned and left for haunted until three years ago. My campsite is already laid and tea is boiling. I make my way across the windy but level ridge and tromp past monastery walls

15th century Jili Dzong on the crest where we will camp
Location: Along Druk's Path, Bhutan

toward the smiling face of Belden. I've never been quite so ready for warmer clothes, a cup of tea, and to stop walking.

As I write this, I am sitting on the ridge amid countless poles strung with prayer flags. It seems that windy ridges are places of choice and the strength of the constant wind will carry prayers to heaven. All over Bhutan you can see rows of prayer flagpoles decorating the hillsides with prayer lists for various blessings. I found an old hand-hewn and painted spire used on top of the poles on the ground near me, and will take it with me in memory of this ancient place. A hot cup of tea does not keep my hands from shaking and the wind is bitter cold coming up the ridge. Despite hat and coat I am very chilled and having difficulty writing.

While I sit facing west, the sun is bright but I am not

Prayer flags along the windswept ridge near Jili Dzong
Location: Druk's Path, Bhutan

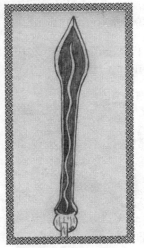

Prayer flag spire

warm. Two young monks from the Dzong walk over cautiously to join me. One speaks some English and asks if this book I am writing in has any pictures in it. I'd never thought of that! What an idea—to carry a picture book of America. Far away places are always awe inspiring, and we forget that our country is a far away place to the rest of the world. They smile, sit on the windy yak-grazed ground and lean against a formidable prayer flagpole, suddenly content to be quiet and just look at me. Feeling self-conscious, I return to writing and wish I had the gift of drawing, as I would like to sketch their faces. They get up to leave and say they will show me the monastery later if I like, and "please you would remove shoes for the temple". But of course.

Evening:

The wind is merciless and in its fury no fire will start, nor will the cook stove ignite. I've put on all my clothes layers and still shiver. But in the fading afternoon light, I make a sparse but adequate nest in my tent and put things where I will find them later in the dark. That essential task completed, I rejoin Kinley and Belden, plus a Japanese hiker and a local yak-herder who have joined us, back out in the wind. The men all talk rapidly in local color, and I know they are discussing weather. They have moved the entire tent in another direction and are busy repositioning tent ties—a sure sign that they expect it to change and be formidable. They will not allow me to help, even after repeated requests. I've certainly done it before. So I sit and continue to be not-very-warm.

Unique among experiences is watching the cook. Once the cook-tent is secured against the wind, he proceeds to move the entire cooking array indoors—including a cast iron wok ring burner hooked to a butane tank. Then he gallantly moved me inside as well, complete with a small side table, chair, candle and tea. Quite

Cook tent set up for Belden's "gourmet kitchen" Location; Druk's Path, Bhutan

frankly I was delighted to be out of the wind, but what followed was amazing. With one burner and no wasted motion, in a space less than 6x8 feet (several of which were occupied by me) Belden proceeded to create a full meal. Now, mind you, I'm not talking the Boy Scout version of camp-out food here. He served up lemon chicken soup, followed by red rice with chili chicken, stir-fry green beans with onions and mushrooms, asparagus in cheese sauce and peeled fresh tomatoes. And, all seasoned to suit the palate of a well-trained chef. It deserved a fine cabernet at the very least. I have a gourmet kitchen, and I am in awe.

We ate while I listened to Dzongkha banter about the price of yak meat and the differences between Japanese and Indian soy sauces. The language is very foreign to my ears, but it was surprising how much I could understand. Occasionally Kinley would interpret a phrase for me, but most of it was that universal form of casual conversation used by people with little connection other than being forced inside the same small room by inclement weather. The Japanese hiker works for the Japanese government and was "on loan" to Bhutan for a month gathering geological survey information. He would camp near us, but be on his way in another direction in the morning. The yak-herder will join us here, taking charge of the pack ponies and helping Belden with the camp. His name is Wongdi, and he does not speak much if at all—with shyness that does not allow him to meet my eye or make any gesture of greeting and his responses to Kinley and Belden are single-syllable and undecipherable. I like him, though, and it is clear he is a friend to the ponies and yaks.

Outside the tent the wind turned to rain and then to snow—and I was assured the morning would be most beautiful. I walked to my tent under the eerie glow of a full moon on glistening snow, on stage between the clouds. There were several yaks in the adjacent meadow dusted with white and watching to be sure I was not headed in their direction. A dog barked nearby, and the soft sounds of the men still talking were the only night sounds to be heard. The stark silhouette of Jili Dzong stood as a fortress against the elements and it was easy to see why it's been called "haunted". The security of my tent is welcome, but the imposing outline of those white walls against the moonlight does not easily fade from memory.

Jili Dzong
by moonlight

I indulge in my solitary ritual with the wildflowers I picked close by, a glass of port to celebrate the day, a lighted candle special for the memories it brings—small pleasures for my mind to dwell on as I court sleep. There is magic here, and memories as clear and crisp as mountain air.

> "Come softly," spoke the Dragon;
> "Walk my ridges, feel my breath
> upon your fragile frame—
> and take from me the light
> of magic memories.
>
> Yet do not take too much of
> what your frail heart can't absorb.
> You must feel the power within,
> for there are many ways
> to touch the face of God."

Creating the ambiance for evening rituals
Location: Druk's Path, Bhutan

April 9, 2001

Morning:

I can see the shapes and shadows inside my tent signaling morning light, and hear the soft sounds of a camp waking up to begin the day. A quiet "Good Morning" is uttered outside the tent door, but I lay still and don't respond—the footsteps retreat softly. I slept, but was conscious of the cold most of the night, and was rejoicing in feeling semi-warm, content to drowse longer and postpone finding out where all the sore and stiff parts are currently located.

I make "tent noises" and it is obvious to my wonderful and attentive crew that I'm alive and moving. A cheerful greeting from outside offers me a cup of tea with sugar and a bowl of hot water with which to wash. Both are most welcome, and the tent is warm enough to enjoy changing into yesterday's dirty clothes over a slightly cleaner body. There is nothing like wilderness hiking to remind me of the many things we take for granted.

I join the men for breakfast—corn flakes, toast and eggs, with Bhutan jam made locally. We share left over toast with an old and emaciated yak dog (all of whom are called *"doshi")*. He walks stiffly, and is uncertain of our kindness, flashing wary looks around but finally hunger overcomes his fears and he gets close enough to eat from the ground near my feet. Kinley's guess is that he got injured on his back leg, was unable to work the herd and was left behind. His condition certainly supports that theory, although his eyes are bright and teeth look good. With some food and care, he would be a beautiful dog—black and tan, reminding me of a Bernese mountain dog only smaller. I hope between the trekkers and the monks he will at least see some comforts for the rest of his days, but I doubt it.

After breakfast while Belden and Wongdi break camp, Kinley and I visit Jili Dzong. We are greeted by the head monk, take our cumbersome laced hiking boots off, and enter the temple. It has been beautifully restored and tended, and one of the loveliest I've seen so far. The monk offers prayers for us, and asks me to light three butter lamps on the altar. I kneel and do so while Kinley says morning prayers. Then the monk pours holy water from the copper urn at the altar into our cupped hands. Following Kinley's lead, I sip from my hands, making a slurping sound and put the rest on my head. There is an awful taste in the water, and much comes to mind concerning its cleanliness but the honorable and respectful thing to do was to sip it. "When in Rome....." and I said a small addendum prayer for sterile water. The taste of it haunted me, however, as I knew I should recognize it and couldn't. It was almost the taste of a perfume that had been added, leaving a metallic and unpleasant taste, yet I could not place it. (I later found out it was "camphor water" (*Aha!*) which accounts for the unique bitter taste and made me feel a little better for having swallowed it several times during temple visits.)

We are told the story of the monastery, how it was built in 1465, then embellished and enlarged in the 1800's. It was left to the villagers to tend, (though where the village is I haven't a clue. All I have seen is one lonely deserted farmstead and a yak-herder's nomadic tent.) Then it fell into disuse and was finally abandoned. Three monks arrived to restore it, and strangely all three died there giving some validity to the legend that it was haunted. No one wanted to risk living there, so it was left to deteriorate for nearly a century. Three years ago a troop of 15 Paro Dzong monks were assigned the duty of moving there and restoring the temple—and they have been at that task ever since. The floors are clean and polished, the altar set grandly, the Bhuddas re-surfaced with gold and the fabric hangings mended and cleaned. They are also painting the frescos and restoring wooden railings and prayer wheels, but the head monk expressed his administrative discontent over lack of funds to do the job properly—a universal challenge we all face that needed no translation. I left a money offering and had Kinley translate for me that I felt I had been privileged to be in this beautiful and holy place, and could feel the peace and respect he and his fellow monks had lovingly restored. He smiled, bowed low, and replied that the monastery would offer prayers for my safe journey and life's happiness tonight at their prayer time. Truly a gift—and I felt very humble.

Young monks in the
temple doorway
Location: Jili Dzong
Druk's Path,
Bhutan

Mid-Morning:

      I stop at the crest between two beautiful ridges. The early hiking was such a pleasure even though the up-hills would not let me forget my limitations. I've added new wildflowers to my hat, and had nearly an hours' walk alone through a dense and moss-covered forest dotted here and there with blooming rhododendrons. A tiny bird, black crested with white on his head and orange underneath caught my attention as he and his mate flitted from branch to branch picking bugs off small rhododendron buds. Seemingly unperturbed by my presence, they got very close, only a few feet away from me at eye level and picked merrily away while carrying on domestic conversation. I watched for nearly five minutes until they opted for another tree on down the trail behind me. Contemplating their easy compatibility, I take the moment to reflect whether or not conjugal bliss is more closely aligned when the topics for

Red rhododendrons
along the trail
Location: Druk's Path, Bhutan

chat are survival—surely we crowd our lives with such complexities that we must ultimately have too much to debate and the chances to live in the moment are too few and far between.

      I soon reach a lovely spot between two stands of ancient trees and catch up to Kinley. He acknowledges my presence as I scramble onto a rather flat rock. The view is spectacular, to the north-northeast, and huge fluffy clouds command the sky and eliminate all possibility of seeing the mountain range beyond these foothills. "Foothills" is indeed a misnomer unless you live in the presence of the Himalayas—they are taller than anything we have for comparison in our hemisphere—and in this part of the world

A view from a flat rock on top of the world
Location: Druk's Path, Bhutan

they don't even name anything unless it's over 16,000 feet.   By now, Kinley believes I am writing a book and chooses to be certain I have plenty of time for it and jokingly asked if I was writing about him, Belden and Wongdi. He naps in the sun, out of eyesight but I know he is just beyond a bush behind me. As I begin to write, a small ant crawls across the blank page, taking my mind back to memories of other mountain tops and spiritual journeys....

The tops of trees play back the
deafening sounds of quiet as the
wind blows gently.
Warm sunlight sends a pattern
on this ridge, where lovers would
stop, breathless, wordless,
and share a chaste embrace—
the only sensuality needed
would be the staggering beauty.

Rhododendron buds

Temporary shelters built
and used by yak herders
for centuries
Location:
Druk's Path, Bhutan

Yak meadows used by yaks for centuries
Location: Druk's Path, Bhutan

Mid-Afternoon:

Through short bursts of "up" I come across a yak meadow and the rock enclosures used by herders. The walls are thigh high of rocks, three sided, with the open side away from prevailing wind. There are rough-hewn poles leaning and scattered in disarray and it is described for me how the nomad herders use this camp every year as they have for centuries. It is a lonely looking place, and I am glad we are not camping here even though sometimes others have camped in the meadow. We hike on and I am glad of a short climb to a wondrously old and magic forest where surely dragons must have lived! JRR Tolkein would have smiled to see a place so close in reality to his fertile imaginations.

There's magic here.
I feel it in the
air and moss that
gently brush my shoulders
as I walk—
careful not to waken
whatever mysteries
are still alive
in this most obvious
of dragon's places.
In such a forest as this,
surely time has walked
more slowly—
and allowed a trace
of magic to remain
for certain lucky
souls to find.

The trail, magical and mystical
in forested places
Location: Druk's Path, Bhutan

I reach the camp—the ponies and the cook are so much faster than I am, so all is prepared. A pair of watchful crows has been following me the last hour and they seem to have taken up temporary residence in the tree near my tent. I change to warmer clothes although tonight we are in a sheltered saddle out of the wind and amid some trees, and at a slightly lower altitude than Jili Dzong. As I stand off by myself and let my muscles unwind, I watch the ponies and their trail bells move softly around the camp waiting to be untacked and turned loose to munch what sparse high meadow grass exists. I seem to have forgotten that I have ever been anywhere else and breathe in the aromatic steam rising from my teacup.

Pack ponies patiently waiting the end of their day's duties Location: Druk's Path, Bhutan

Evening:

Belden calls me to dinner and I find the snowfall I've been listening to so softly on my tent has made the world white. The ponies, still grazing around the camp, are now covered with a blanket of snow and look like horse-shaped versions of flocked Christmas trees. It is cold, but it is very beautiful. Kinley assures me that it will snow all night and we are likely to awake to a winter wonderland and will have to dig out of it to continue on the trail.

The meal is another culinary *fait 'a compli.* I was handed a bowl of steaming hot cream of mushroom soup and then served dumplings, which they call *"momo"*. These are hand-made of minced chicken and pork, onions, seasonings and rolled in round wheat dough twisted and pinched on top with the skill of a trained pastry chef. Unable to resist I ate too many and then had to suffer through rice/wheat stir fry topped with potatoes, carrots, green beans and onions—then tea and canned sweet cherries for dessert. I am served alone with Kinley offering polite company. Kinley is very intelligent and a lively conversationalist. We talked of many things while I ate and I enjoyed his wit and opinions. I asked why they were not all going to join me at dinner, and he indicated that the men would eat together after I was "taken care of". I shared with him that I felt a little awkward about being waited on so obviously, and that I was willing and capable of doing my part of the camp chores. He merely said, "But you are our guest—and guests must be treated with the greatest respect." They each seem so cheerful and relaxed with the process that I began to understand it is a gift they give me rather than an expectation they must meet. How far we have come from graciousness in our culture—I had to have it explained to me before I could grasp it.

On the edge of darkness, I make my way through a full ground cover of snow and worm into my sleeping bag for warmth. We are to leave very early tomorrow with the hope of seeing early morning signs of wildlife. Also, tomorrow is the longest day over two high passes to the campsite near a trout lake and I will need much of it to get there before late afternoon.

The little sanctuary of my tent seems miles away from the real world, and I'm allowing myself the stillness it takes to really examine the delicacy of a purple-blue mountain wildflower. A sip of port to celebrate another day near the heart of the Dragon—and before I sleep I'll let the soft flame of this candle clear my mind of everything but the burning flame it represents.

In the dead and dark silence of night the snow has stopped falling. A pheasant who was sheltered underneath a nearby tree suddenly flutters, and moves to change his location—his small space of security disrupted by a sound I cannot hear. Then soft footsteps pass my tent, the rhythmic even steps of bi-pedal walking, arousing all my senses to full alert and I listen. The soft steps move away, on down the hill, some other purpose pursued. As I lay quietly, listening with all my body, the dead dark silence sets in again and the distant tinkle of a pony's neck bell pierces the quiet. Suddenly, the stories and bravado about being Yeti bait aren't quite so funny. Be careful what you wish for!

April 10, 2001

I am greeted with a cheery good morning and asked if I'm ready for tea. Belden brushes snow from my tent and hands me a steaming cup. The sun is out, but the camp is surrounded by eye-level clouds. From my tent door, I see that shimmering winter wonderland the storm had promised. Time to be up and off.

Overnight snow storm brings a winter wonderland
to the difficult terrain
Location: Druk's Path, Bhutan

Lively and pointed discussion is taking place near the cook tent. During breakfast I'm informed that the snow makes it dangerous to take the ponies over the high passes. They will have to back track and take a shorter, lower trail to another campsite at a lower lake than the one designated on our route. I am given the option of taking that same route, or taking the higher ridge route. Kinley is careful to point out that the higher route is the most demanding, and due to the change, it would add two to two and a half hours of hiking to an already difficult day—but it was the true Druk's Path. He left me to ponder and said it was up to me to decide. Part of me opted for the easier day. After all, I'm still on this hike for me, I don't need to impress anyone and besides who would know the difference? It occurred to me that I'd be better off following the ponies, safer if anything happened, and I debated with myself over the sanity of choosing difficulty.

But the sun was out, the snow beautiful, and my desire to finish what I started and make the journey all the way prevailed. And from somewhere inside, my inner voice wondered what the Dragon would think? I told Kinley I wanted to take the high road and he said, "Then let's get going. And there won't be time for stopping to write today if we wish to make camp by dark." He had my attention. I moved quickly.

Evening:

Kinley was right, there was no writing or resting time this entire day. And as I recount this, I realize I *have* been writing all day in my head. So many things I would have committed to paper if I stopped to do it—turns of phrase, descriptions of beauty, even explosions of poetry that will never attend the surface of my conscious mind again and unfortunately are lost. I always seem to have the most brilliant moments of literary genius when I'm unable to write it down! So who would ever believe me? Well, I will at least attempt to capture the day and perhaps, a few great moments will find their way to the pages of my journal.

We leave camp headed through virgin snow, gently treading on the hill that sheltered us overnight. The morning air is crisp and sun shines through the haze of treetop clouds. I'm exhilarated, proud of myself for not giving in to the temptation of an easier route. And I will pay for that later.

Kinley had asked Belden and Wongdi to keep a lookout for a good walking stick for me, since I disliked his aluminum one and wanted a real piece of wood from the mountain. Each of them found one, and each had carefully stripped off knubs and thorns to make it smooth and easy to handle. One is tall and straight, the other short with a cane-like handle and a bit of character. I thanked them both, and so as not to play favorites, decided to take them both and use them. It was awkward at first, but I soon kicked into a cross-country ski rhythm and they worked. I had no idea how valuable they would both become, and how I literally would depend on them to finish this day on my feet. Hoping to see wildlife, we left the other hiker camped downhill

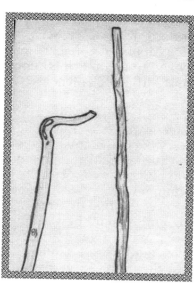

Walking Sticks: Tall one made by Belden, and short one made by Wongdi

and hoped we had a couple hours before he overtook, passed, and made enough noise to scare away any local inhabitants. We saw rock pheasant, monal, and deer tracks but nothing more.

Rock Pheasant
and feather

   Kinley knew the trail and our footprints through the new snow made it easy for the followers to catch up. The man who had camped nearby caught up to me and gave a good morning greeting. He was from San Francisco and wasted no time telling me he'd been on a trek to Mt. Everest base camp last week, so this "was just a stroll" for him. I thanked him for that kind thought, and told him that this was an accomplishment for me. I gladly let him go on ahead and was pleased he chose to remain solitary. Kinley is unimpressed, and we've been rather sarcastically referring to him as "Joe Mountain Climber" ever since. He appeared to lack sensitivity and wasn't much for encouraging words for a fellow hiker on a most difficult challenge!
   We hike up. It seems as though there is no other way but "up". I find I am still easily winded and have to stop frequently to catch my breath. Today the trail rarely dips below 10,000 feet, and every red cell in my body is working overtime to keep enough oxygen available for straining muscles. It's funny the games your mind will play with your body to keep it from damage and crisis. When I stop, my heart races, the pulse pounds in my ears and I'm close to hyperventilating to catch my breath. Unbidden and unconsciously I begin to count how many breaths go with four pounding heartbeats. When I get down to one, then I count how many breaths it takes until I can no longer feel the pulse in my ears. As my heart rate slows and I can take two or three deep breaths calmly, I start walking again. I decided my treadmill is really a blessing rather

than a curse; but one thing is for certain—the strain of the altitude sure does keep your mind focused on the physical needs of the moment.

I come to a ridge, a beautiful level walk through a sun-drenched scrub forest. Kinley walks ahead and leaves me to my silent thoughts. It seems the ridge is truly the back of the dragon and as I look back, I can see it stretch off and down, with rock out-croppings that look like scales. As I look forward, I can see his

The Dragon's Back Ridge
Location: Druk's Path, Bhutan

head curl to face the mountain peak Jhomolhari, the tallest in Bhutan and the fifth tallest in the Himalayan range. The famous mountain shrouds itself in cloud cover and will not show itself to me on this trip. It is as if my Dragon is saying, "You must pay attention to me."

> The sultry dragon lies
> sleepy in the sun,
> one eye half-closed
> but watchful.
> The tiny intruder
> on his back,
> intent on sights
> and sounds and
> lofty heights
> is unaware of
> such close scrutiny.
> And so the skies cloud,
> the wind screams,
> the trees bend and bow—
> and blinking one great eye,
> the dragon reminds me
> where I am.

I struggle to reach the third of the high passes and the vertical climb is so demanding that Kinley is hovering closely. After asking repeatedly, he finally insists on taking my small backpack. I shed my Super Woman pelt and give it up and feel better, but guilty. The top is crowned with the Buddhist version of a trail duck—a laptse—which is a large pile of rocks serving several purposes, among which are to mark the trail in the snow and to appease

Lha Gyal Lo!
Location: Druk's Path, Bhutan

the local deities. Travelers add to the stone pile and say "Lha Gyal Lo" or "May the gods prevail," out of respect for the gods—which seems like a very good idea to me. Kinley has been watching the skies and I recognize snow clouds hovering heavily in the space between the ridges we are crossing. He is unconsciously hurrying me and I sense his urgency as we have a very long way to go and it appears to be well past midday.

After much up and down, we finally arrive at a very beautiful glacial-fed trout lake. I had been hearing water for some time and discover it is the spillway into the narrow valley that I have just circumvented. This is where we would have camped if it had not snowed so heavily and been dangerous for the ponies. Knowing that, I have the first of some very qualified negative thoughts: Why am I doing this exactly? What do I have to prove? Who's idea was this anyway and why didn't I take the shorter route? I'm cold, tired, my boots are beginning to soak through and we still have more than two hours to hike, three, in my case, since I'm slow. I am not hungry but Kinley insists I eat a couple of dry fish sandwiches and drink juice. He's right of course, but it doesn't taste good and the over-exertion and dehydration has begun to give me a headache.

A difficult, steep, snow and ice ascent out of the high lake valley
Location: Druk's Path, Bhutan

That little rest is short-lived and since of course the lake was "down", we now have to head "up". Again. It is mid-afternoon and the snow has melted trickling down the trail and leaving slippery mud all over its path of least resistance which neatly also happens to coincide with my trail. No surprise there. Every step is a study in how to avoid an ankle deep puddle of muddy water which is very exhausting. My neck and shoulders are tensed, balancing for each step, and making my headache a real pain. I don't even remember how many up-down-ups we did for the next couple hours, but finally Kinley said, "This is the last stretch, a nice gentle down to another lake that I can see in the distance." He even points out where the camp is, and I spot the green tent belonging to Joe Mountain Climber. Several uncharitable thoughts come to mind and I maintain enough dignity to keep them to myself. Unprepared for the amount of snow that fell this time of the year, Kinley had no gaiters and his feet were wet and nearly frozen. He asks if I'm OK to hike alone since he needs to get to camp and dry his feet before the cold causes damage. Once again, I find myself grateful for having gotten good gear—my feet are wet but warm, and the boots and socks that seemed such an extravagance in San Diego are truly a necessity here. I assure him I'm fine (although privately admitting to myself I'm <u>not</u> fine, I'm cold, I'm tired, I'm hungry, I'm pretty miserable, I'm fed up with this surly Dragon) and tell him to please go on ahead and I'll be there shortly.

Actually being able to see the camp far below makes it so I didn't have to be quite so much of a liar.

Setting a pace and using my walking sticks which have become a necessity, I make my way downhill. My legs are tired and that accentuates the pounding on my knee joints—but I'm now feeling "the end of the day" adrenaline kick in, spawned by the knowledge that Belden has hot tea waiting. I catch myself hurrying and slip on a wet rock twisting my ankle just enough to bring a few randomly chosen words to my lips. Back to my pace, the one that works so well.

I hear the sound of a neck bell every so often, and finally stop to listen. All the ponies have long since made it to camp and this sound seems to be behind me. It stops when I stop, and then as I walk on I hear it again and wonder if I'm hearing it echoing up from camp. But no, there it is again, and I'm certain it is behind me. I stop again and turn around—and sure enough, a big black yak comes around the corner behind me with his neck bell jangling in time to his uneven, rocking pace. He stops and watches me watch him. No doubt he roamed a little off course for I don't see any others. I fumble with coat zippers and pockets trying to find my camera impeded by the slowness of freezing fingers. But he is not interested in my moment of triumphant satisfaction, and leaves

My
Yak trail
partner

the trail headed for high ground and snowed-in meadows. Who is to say if I really ever saw him? But I think he was my yak trekking partner—or perhaps a Himalayan angel.

I reach camp, greeted with smiles and scalding hot tea. Once again I burn my mouth and simultaneously curse the damaged taste buds and praise the fact that it's been boiled so well. I'm so tired I sit by the campfire somewhat dazed, listening to the Bhutanese banter as the men dry socks and shoes and pile more wood on and start preparing dinner. I am not hungry; in fact, the idea of eating makes me a little queasy. But I manage hot soup and a meat pastry, and a few bites from a bowl of rice that would serve four. Belden again outdoes what should be camp fare, and I feel so impolite to leave it—but more would be a mistake. I'm so cold, dusk is long past, and I'm ready to be alone for a while and see if I can make sense of this day.

As I lie here writing, I find myself staring at the candle and thinking that even the sip of port is unappealing. There is poetry in this—but I am too tired and cold to find it. I will crawl into my sleeping bag, wearing all my clothes, and hope the shivering will stop long enough to sleep. No more writing, but I think I'll watch the candle a little longer. . .

April 11, 2001:

Morning:

Kinley said he would wake me at sunrise so we could beat Joe Mountain Climber to the trail and see whatever wildlife there may be. I am stiff and cold, have not slept well, and as I hear the early morning stirring of camp sounds I secretly hope his wake up call will be a while yet.

Without ceremony I find hot tea outside my tent and warm water for washing. Together they create what passes for warmth and the sunlight shines through my tent door. It actually warms my small space just barely enough to coax me into the day.

Mid-Morning:

We have been hiking several hours now, and the "ups" are more gradual and there is a welcome mix of a few "levels" to help me out. Kinley has been on sharp lookout for critters (while I watch my feet—I can't seem to look and walk at the same time in this terrain). All we see are tracks, but they are varied and many in the early morning virgin snow. We saw the carefully placed footprints of deer of various sizes, pheasants, a probable pika, and even a smallish hunting cat who preferred our trail and led on before us for quite a way before taking off into the brush. The cat left the trail to inspect a small laptsa to the west and marked it, with little regard

A place to "mark the trail," in more ways than one! Location: Druk's Path, Bhutan

for respect—then headed off into the dwarf rhododendron under-brush. It occurs to me that the gods must have a well developed sense of humor and his social commentary is logged in much the same way as the small rocks left by travelers.

The day is beautiful; sky of deepest blue, crisp cold air and all the mountains in a new blanket of searing frosty white. I have thoughts of simple things, my garden at home, a spring picnic, wondering what wildflowers may appear—there have been none visible since the snowfall, and I am missing them.

Mid-Afternoon:

I hike alone for much of the day which is a special treat, and I seem to have found an easy pace or else I'm getting a little tougher and it really is easier. I am in awe of the beauty and stop more now to gaze at the 360-degree views rather than to catch my breath. The mountains—some of my soul definitely resides here. The quiet time alone pushes away the façade and leaves room for a sudden flood of memories:

A box, tied neatly with red ribbons
appears unbidden out of storage.
Knowing full well the contents,
the tightly tied knots unravel,
letting memories drift upwards
to consciousness. And before
I can slam the lid and keep things
where they belong, the soft gray ghosts
of long forgotten memories rise
to mingle with the mists and clouds.

The highest point on the trail - Phume La
at 4210m/13,812 feet!
Location: Druk's Path, Bhutan

Today we reach the highest point on the trek, Phume La, at 4210 meters "to be exact" as Kinley says. There is a large laptse at the crest and we take pictures as I add my rock to the very top. Hillary's got nothin' on me, baby! And as I catch my breath at this highest of places, a special rock catches my eye. Rocks find you, you don't find them. I pick it up and put it in my pocket to bring back with me—a small scale from the back of my Dragon as a token of remembrance—and somehow I know he doesn't mind.

The rest of the way to camp is down and level but we still
have several hours of hiking ahead. Kinley and I chat amiably and
I discover he likes Kenny Rogers, Garth Brooks and Elvis music.
We compare families and I learn that he and Belden have children,
but he's not sure about Wongdi. I tell him about my trip on a cattle drive in Montana and we agree he'll send me some seeds for the
little hot red chilies I've gotten fond of eating with them on this
trip. The time passes and again he allows me the solitude of an
hour's stretch over the last of the high country yak meadows. I can
feel the age of this place. Rock walls used as tent shelters, earth
pounded hard and bare with centuries of yak and horse hooves,
mountains covered with threatening, heavy snow clouds. The
winds pick up and it turns from pleasant to cold and my feet are
now wet from melted snow puddles I was unable to miss. Off in
the distance the Dragon wakes and a soft but determined roll of
Dragon thunder can be heard. Snow begins to fall. I catch up to
Kinley and we walk with purpose. We can see the monastery where
we will camp, but it is still far below and the snow begins in
earnest.

Rolls of thunder; my Dragon speaks loudly, congratulating
me on success. For some strange reason amid thick swirls of snow
and thundering clouds and downhill mud, my eyes fill with tears
and I have to stop as they roll uncontrollably down my cheeks.
Luckily, Kinley is enough ahead of me that I am able to compose
myself before he notices. He would misinterpret—and I would be
unable to explain the emotions generated by the soft, sultry, powerful voice of this mountain Dragon.

Evening:

What happened next I can hardly describe to give it proper
dimension and visualization. The snow began to fall, wet and
heavy, and the Dragon made his point quite clearly. Kinley began
to get a little concerned since below us he could see an unfamiliar
tent amid the several buildings of the large monastery Phajoding
Goemba, where we are to camp—but not ours. He was worried they
might have gone on farther and that could leave us stranded in this
gathering storm. His usual peaceful and serene countenance was
marked with concern, and I knew him well enough by now to recognize the small but perceptible changes in the set of his jaw and
the demand in his step.

The fog and blowing snow had all the promise of an impending blizzard and the shapes of the buildings below grew misty and undefined. As we got closer, all of a sudden Belden appeared from the shapeless doorway of one of the buildings and waved us to go there. It seems that his wife's uncle is a sort of stores-caretaker for the monks of the monastery and with that connection, Belden was able to arrange special permission for me to stay inside the protection of the monastery walls since the weather was bad and everyone was tired and cold. I had learned that women were not allowed in monasteries from sunset to sunrise and asked if this was appropriate. Belden's uncle had sent a young monk messenger up to the meditation temple at the top of the ridge overlooking the monastery courtyard, asking the head lama for spe-

Phajoding Goempa Monastery - looking down
through the pending storm where I spent the night
Location: On the last stretch of Druk's Path, Bhutan

cial permission for a lone woman traveler to be inside overnight. He gave his gracious permission since the lower building was designated as a teaching monastery and I must remain in the dzong containing the dormitories for students.

We entered through the huge wooden doors open to the world during the day, and into the centuries old stone courtyard of the monastery. The temple wall opposite was multi-storied, and towered over the square which housed the monks, the students, the classrooms and the caretakers in tiny rooms. I was ushered upstairs to the second story off the courtyard and into the uncle's one-room home. Inside, there was a wood burning stove and hot tea waiting for me. The room was very small, very used, and smelled of damp wool, old spices, musty wood, with the distinctive odor of a place inhabited only by men for hundreds of years. I was offered a place of honor to sit while everyone else sat on the floor—and that place was the pallet that was this man's bed. He had spread it with as many rugs and hides as he possessed, and shook the yak hide on top (complete with bald spots from age and vermin) to make it smooth for me. Knowing what probably lives in old yak hides, my instincts were to recoil, but how could anyone deny this most gracious hospitality? This man was offering me his only personal space in the world, as if it were a throne. Never before have I been gifted with something so small that meant so much. The uncle was shy, and after that welcoming gesture I never saw him again. The fire felt so good and true to some unwritten law of hearths the world over, a small calico cat lay with paws curled under its chest and eyes half open soaking up the heat, arrogantly unconcerned with the rest of the world.

        After warming myself near the stove with several cups of tea, I was escorted to the other side of the courtyard to the room where I would be allowed to sleep. My gallant cook and yak herder were obviously concerned that I might find the accommodations distasteful, and Belden and Wongdi had spent considerable time cleaning the room before I arrived. They had laid a huge tarp and mats on the floor and the wood smelled of fresh soap and water— they had actually washed the floor for me! I was profuse in my appreciation and was left to sort out my things and put on dry clothes. Kinley suggested it might be "a good time to write more of your book" while they prepared dinner. I was delighted and began arranging my "nest". The room was about 6X6 square with

Dormitory
windows,
looking out of
my room to
the courtyard
Phajoding
Goempa
Monastery

a wooden door and walls of centuries-old slats covered with magazine pages and newspapers as insulation against the wind. A box of six windowpanes filled the wall that faced into the courtyard and the light bounding off the clouded sky against the whitewashed walls of the temple cast plenty of light into the room. With my back to the windows, I settled about looking for something dry to put on that I could tolerate. As I riffled through my pack, the room got suddenly dark. I turned around to see my windows blocked by the faces of 15-20 young monks, all peering through the windows and giggling. Finally one was chosen for the "dare" and pushed into my doorway. He spoke softly, *"kuzozangpo la"*—the respectful form of "hello" and I returned the bow and greeting, smiling. Then, in heavily accented English, he said, "We wish to know please, are you really a girl?" I smiled and answered yes, which ignited another huge ripple of giggling. He bowed ever so politely saying *"kadinchey la"* (thank you, respectfully) and just then a stern and deep voice could be heard, shooing the boys and obviously scolding them for dallying on their way to temple. An older monk, most likely a teacher, entered the open doorway and apologized in Dzongkha for this bad behavior and then asked if he could light his fist full of incense sticks on my candle. I indicated he could, of course, and the pungent, aromatic smoke filled my small room. He waved them around with a quiet chant—and even now I'm not certain whether he was blessing me or cleansing the room of the evil spirit of a woman among his young students.

Kinley brings me tea and I am invited to watch dinner preparations. I walk back over to the uncle's room, glad to be near the stove again, and the men are making *"momo"*, those meat-filled dumplings very like pilimeni. Kinley and Belden work deftly amid chaos and pans and dirt and age—and I am quite impressed at how cleanly they accomplish this "hands-on" cooking under such conditions. They are obviously skilled and hygienically educated about food preparation, and their workspace is a sterile field. Wongdi is apparently the gopher, and comes and goes as instructed with one syllable replies. He avoids eye contact with me but when it happens accidentally he smiles shyly. Belden barks orders congenially and Wongdi washes a pan in hot soapy water. But then he dries it unobserved with a towel hung on a nail near the door unwashed since the dawn of time. I cringe, and decide that I'm close enough to getting back to the world of western medicine that

I can probably survive anything for 24 more hours. I am instructed verbally on how to prepare, fold and cook momo and also given
several suggestions on how to serve and eat it. Fascinated, I promised to try it at home and report how it turns out. The secret is the
cooking pan—a large four tiered aluminum steamer, and they tell
me I can find one just like Belden's in Thimphu. The rest is prac-
tice.

    The *momo* and cabbage soup are so good that I eat until I'm
completely stuffed. More tea, some fruit and sweet biscuits for
dessert, and then I'm escorted back to my room across the square.
Belden gives me extra candles to write by and as I lay here, warm
in my sleeping bag, I listen to monks chant in the temple room near
me. Their prayers increase in fervor and tempo, and soon drums
and cymbals and bells add to the program. It is mystical and
unearthly sounding and discordant to my western ears. If you
listen closely it is repeated phrases, but that too is difficult to discern. Then, all at once, it stops—silence. I am in a very foreign,
mysterious and unknown place; a place where I have been given

My room at
Phajoding
Goempa
Monastery,
overlooking the
temple
courtyard.

grace to stay but am not allowed, a place where the world stands still and time is of no consequence. A dog barks, a young student's voice practices a prayer close to the wall of my room, soft laughter from a lighted room across the courtyard, the unmistakable hoot of a large owl drift on the winds of the silence. I am, without doubt, in the heartbeat of an adventure.

Physiology being what it is, before I settle down to sleep I must make my way outside the walls of the courtyard to the latrine tent. Being female, my options are more limited than the "over the rail" technique used by the monks. It was pitched a rather fair walk from the doors of the monastery, and I attempt to push open the huge wooden doors without attracting attention. They creak and groan mercilessly and sound like the drawbridge of a medieval castle being lowered over the moat. Standing in the doorway of this walled-in sanctuary I look out and can see the light of Thimphu a long way below in the valley, and realize I am ready to go back to life as I usually live it. With careful steps, I stumble toward the shadow of the tent, using a small flashlight that only succeeds in keeping me from falling over a dog curled up against the wind. He growls a half-hearted protest at the intrusion and I continue onwards. There are others outside, and the imposing shape of the monastery walls loom behind me ominously. My nerves are attentive. On the way back, I am met by Kinley who politely admonishes me, saying I should ask him to accompany me if I need to leave my room again during the night. I assure him that I'll stay inside until morning. He walks with me to my room, and shows me the bent nail on the inside of the door that serves as a latch, asking me to twist it closed when he leaves since the monastery dogs roam at night and would enjoy curling up on my soft sleeping bag. Then he pulls the door shut and wishes me good night. It seems odd that he would perceive a safety issue, and it leaves me somewhat disconcerted as I move to obey his request and twist the rusty nail into position as a latch.

Middle of Night:

It is clear to me I will not sleep. The noises in the walls are unnerving and despite my fatigue I am wakeful. I put out the candles and flashlight and realize that for the first time this trip, I am actually comfortably warm in the sleeping bag. I hear a noise in the

far corner of the room, think of mice, and pull the flashlight close
to my head for easy access. I must have drifted off for a few minutes despite strange sounds, because I dreamed I was negotiating
for a better hotel room, one with a private bath and large bathtub.
Not too difficult to interpret the meaning in that, as I'm long over-
due for some comfort and cleanliness.

I lie on my left side, which is most comfortable, and look
out the six-panel window to the courtyard and the front of the temple wall. The moon, though no longer full, is very bright in a clear
sky and lights up the whitewashed walls in ghostly light. It's a little scary here—remote, mysterious, ancient. I have no trouble
imagining all sorts of stories and dramas, leaving me feeling alone
and vulnerable in a strange land. Amid these reveries I wonder
what would attract a young boy to this austere life of subsistence
and resignation? They come here so young, anywhere from age
5-6 to 9-10, and I am told that in generations past parents decided
which male child in the family would be a monk, but today it is the
child's decision. An older boy, a young man of age feeling "called"
perhaps—but a six year old?? I cannot quite embrace that, and
again realize how little I understand religion and its compulsion on
the lives of some people. In a world full of so much to see, to learn,
to experience, I cannot imagine choosing such isolation.

Having my back to the marauding mice bothers me, and as
I readjust positions I hear "larger-than-mice" sounds between the
tarp and the wall near my head. This proves too much, so I sit up
and light my candles in an effort to face whatever it is that shares
my room. I hear sounds, not like ones I'm familiar with, and more
like tiny kittens than anything else. Could be, I guess, with several "*bjili*" around. Whoever it is crawls in and out of the wall space
and the possibility of sleep is over. Rats come to mind, although I
have mentally agreed with my fertile imagination that it would be
mice—but maybe not—and an entire microbial scenario unfolds
before me that my hefty set of vaccinations doesn't even begin to
address. I can see by the position of the moon that the night is still
a long way from over and I decide to leave the candles on and settle down to wait it out, alert, awake, and with nerves on edge.

In the dark before dawn, I hear someone come through the
huge creaky gate. I quickly blow out my candles knowing that if
someone saw light in my windows they might worry that I was OK
at that hour, and I did not wish to cause anyone concern. Soft footsteps (our hiking boots make distinctly different noises than the

monks' soft slipper shoes) make their way across the courtyard and up the wooden stairs to the walkway near my room. The silence persists several minutes and just as my breathing begins again, a gong sounds and sends me nearly a foot off the ground. I feel the floorboards vibrate under me as I sit there, stunned by the sudden noise, hearing it reverberate for a long time. It clangs again; then again, in successively more rapid beats until it is a solid ringing and I cover my ears it is so loud. No one stirs—not a soul, not a cough or a groan or a board creaking—and what it signified or called for was unclear to me. Then just as I relaxed into a normal cardiac rhythm again about ten minutes later, the gong repeats its summons in the same manner and all at once the monastery comes alive. I can hear young boys making sleepy movements to the railing outside their rooms, urinating over the sides into the courtyard. Shuffling feet begin to migrate toward the temple near me and soft voices whine their protest at being pushed into the day. Cook pots clang and the occasional dog barks, the wooden floorboards creak in protest as feet make their way to common destinations. Chants begin, morning prayers are raised to heaven in youthful unison, and the sun peaks over the horizon. I am left to conclude that the first gong symphony is simply the "snooze alarm" and the second one means business!

April 12, 2001:

Morning:

Well, whatever lives in the walls stayed there, and is now curled up sleeping so it will be rested and ready to harass tonight's occupant of this room. I'm feeling glad it will not be me. It is full light now and I can see the courtyard come alive with monks of various ages, all in dull red robes wrapped against the cold moving about with their assigned tasks. Across the way the door is open to Belden's cooking kitchen/uncle's room and I know he will be bringing hot tea and breakfast soon.

After breakfast I pack up my things and leave them in the room for Wongdi to carry to the pack horses as instructed. Standing in the doorway, I look around and bid good-bye to the most unusual place I've ever spent the night. The sun shining through the windows leaves partial shadows on the walls and floor. It is stark and bare, ancient, and full of stories and I contemplate the number of

people who have lived in this room over the centuries. Surely the
shadow of my presence for one night, a foreign woman emanating
anxiety and awe, will remain as one of the secrets the walls have
kept. As I slowly close the door, it occurs to me I've just participated in the history of the world. It is a humbling thought.

Kinley collects me for a tour of this huge teaching
monastery and the temples above us on the hill. There are many
buildings in this complex, several caretaker houses, three temples
joined together by two large open courtyards, and above all that a
reclusive house where the head *lama* is now sequestered in meditation. The temples may be visited, but the meditation house is off
limits to everyone but monastery messengers. The first temple has
been in use since 800 AD and the *lama* stops to worship there. It
is only 100 yards from where I slept. Then we hike up a very steep
hill to see two others, both built in the 15th century and also still
being used. A young monk who appears to be in his 20's escorts
us, a large ring of keys jangling in his hand as we cross the stone
walkway to the temple entrance. It is not very different from the
other temples I have been in, and once again, we light butter candles and I leave an offering on the altar. As we leave, he and Kinley
engage in conversation that sounds to me like they are politely
arguing, but Kinley finally bows slightly and we sit to put on our
boots. The monk leaves and enters a side building and Kinley quietly tells me in a slightly sarcastic tone that we will not be able to
see the third temple. Westerners are not allowed in there as there
are artifacts and things that are sacred. Then, as we are lacing up
our boots the monk with the keys opens a shutter and leans out a
window above us and speaks to Kinley. Kinley looks at me and
says, "He tells me that they have made an exception and he will
show you the temple because you have good karma." We unlace
our boots. He says, with one eyebrow raised ever so slightly, that
I'm the first person he's ever had on one of his treks who has been
allowed into that temple. I secretly wonder if *he* believes I have
good karma! Then he tells me that when they dug the foundation
of the temple, in the 1400's, they found a petrified dragon's egg—
a sacred sign of good karma, and that the egg is still there. Kinley
flashes a look that says, '*You don't really believe that, do you?*' but
I scarcely hear or see him and my mouth is hanging open.

We enter the temple and for the first time I see actual scrolls
of religious doctrine, some on long cloths rolled up like a Torah,
some on rice paper bound in leather and wrapped in sack cloth like

a Bible. It makes sense this being a teaching monastery, but I had not seen written documents of doctrine before. The monk inclines his head toward the altar, where Kinley stops to offer prayers and I light butter candles and leave another offering. We receive the ritual of holy water from the monk and then are ushered into a side alcove. A shrine sits off to the side lit by candles, and there sits a large, rusty-gold mottled egg on a golden egg cup. He bows low and tells us this is a dragon's egg and the temple sits on the very spot where it was dug from the earth nearly 1300 years ago. Chills run over my spine and the hair on my neck and arms stands up. I stand in awe—what else can I say? For me, there is no doubt. I believe it *must* be the egg of a dragon.

The Dragon's Egg
in a gold chalice

In deep thought, I walk back to the dormitory building and a raven lands just in front of me on the trail—a good omen to the Bhutanese, and a sign of good fortune. Perhaps, at this particular time in my life, I really do have good karma.

Raven's head
and feathers

Young boy
monks
of Phajoding Goempa
Monastery

We say good-bye to a cluster of boy-monks hanging around giggling and watching us pack up. I take pictures of the three men who attended me on this adventure, not wanting to miss a shot of

L-R: Belden, Kinley and Wongdi
Our last day on the trail as we
leave Phajoding Goempa Monastery

them together in case it is hectic at the end of the trail. Kinley told them I was writing a book and maybe they'd all have their picture in it. They smile, little knowing how right he was, and I smile back and hope that they enjoyed my company as well. (And gentlemen, I hope perhaps you'll read this someday.)

The big hike down is sunny and warm. We make good time, and come upon a large stupa overlooking the Thimphu Valley—reverently honoring departed souls, and strewn with prayer flags left by travelers. I fill my hat with flowers once again and begin to look forward to a reunion with civilization. I take a moment to sit near a small trickle of water down the rocky creek.

The sun warms my face as I write one last time in this journal that has become a catalog of my thoughts and a window to my soul. Silent reflection makes me realize that even my small array of words cannot possibly describe the experience completely, that much of it will be left forever in my memory, unable to be articulated. From here I can't see the ridge that is Druk's Path, but I know he is watching with one eye half open as I leave the mystery of his world and re-enter the mystery of mine. I am looking forward to seeing smiling and familiar faces as I hike these last few miles—I hope they will be there waiting for me at the end of this morning's hike into the city of Thimphu.

Stupa on the ridge overlooking the descent into Thimphu Valley
Location: Druk's Path, Bhutan

Trail's End:

I enter the outskirts of Thimphu and Kinley points out where we end our trip and asks if my friends are going to meet me. I say yes, I know they'll be there. But from a distance I can see no cars in the small parking lot near a youth center. They are expecting me to be there between 11:00am and 12:00 noon, and it is nearly 12:00 noon—so I continue to watch for signs of their arrival. The closer we get I lose confidence and as we reach the parking lot I am deflated completely. This trek was so strenuous, so demanding for me, that I was counting on them all to show up and congratulate me. High fives, cheery smiles, hugs—I guess I hadn't realized how important that final element of closure would be for me, the celebration, the acknowledgment of my success. It feels like winning a gold medal in the Olympics and having no one there to notice and cheer for you. I'm sitting here waiting, alone, and had not imagined it might "end" so unceremoniously. In my sadness, I am reminded of a powerful lesson—when you set expectations, there are disappointments. *C'est la vie*—I'll survive. I always do.

And finally there they are; the adventure is at an end. Kinley presents me with a silk prayer shawl as congratulations and a token of honor. I say my good-byes and realize my disposition will be greatly improved with a hot bath and cold glass of wine.

Goodbyes at the end of the adventure
Location: Thimphu, Bhutan

Epilogue

Trek hat and silk Prayer shawl - a
gift of honor and respect, given at the
end of my journey by
Kinley, Belden and Wongdi

There are things that happen in life—some you choose,
some you don't—which change the fabric of who you are. A tiny
new strand of color, woven into the pattern making it different
somehow, more complex, more intricate, more interesting. Being
alone on the challenge of the Dragon's Back was one of those
things for me.

Burned in my memory are so many things. Prayer flags
overlooking Paro Valley, the early morning virgin snows, a starving
but grateful *"doshi,"* the sound of a lonely yak bell, centuries old

gilded temples, a half-sleeping "*bjili*" under a wood burning stove in a monastery cell. It will take years to sort, to file, to assimilate all the images into that strand of color that is now part of my soul.

Why did I go? I can't be sure—many reasons probably. To prove I could do it? Perhaps. For the solitude and peace the mountains bring me? Partly. Because it's called "Druk's Path"? Seems reasonable. So I could tell the story? Of course. For the satisfaction of feeding my untamed soul, my wild side? No doubt. I can't say for certain. Most likely, it was all of these.

The epiphany, however, was in what I thought about—or rather, what I *didn't* think about. It occurs to me that when you put yourself in the demands of physical challenge, your mind responds by sifting through all the clutter of things that life as we know it contains. It sorts through the sensory overload and leaves you with what you value, what you believe, what you love, who you are.

I thought about challenges: being the best at something, at anything, and I realized that while I'm good at lots of things, I don't have the discipline to ever be "the best" at any one thing. There is too much to experience, too much to try—but the sacrifice for variety is mediocrity, and I must accept the fact that I'll never know the honor or humility of being *number one*, of being *the best*.

I thought about memories: the burden and the joy they bring, and I realized that while I tend to bury them deeply, they are all still there packed neatly on shelves and card-catalogued in the labyrinth library of my mind. Some are good, some are not. And even though some are no longer painful, I also know they have no place close to the surface of my consciousness and should not be allowed out of their boxes. Once the lessons are learned, the book is best left on the shelf.

I thought about relationships: how strange they are, how much they mold the masks that I so carefully wear. With the wisdom that comes with getting older, one would think relationships would have more wisdom, be more easily maintained. Not true. They get more complicated, more incomprehensible. And while I value solitude and the peace of personal space, I realized I was never meant to live alone and would be most unhappy if left to rely on my own company. The value of women friendships grows stronger, and the intimacy of a male partner and lover is mandatory—my soul would starve without both.

I thought about children: not the "worried mother" thoughts I always have in real life, but the re-call of young memories, how dear to me they all were as small children, and yet how easy it is for me to let them fly. I wonder how they will think of me as I grow old? I see so much of myself in each one's personality, whether they like it or not, and hope as life lands with both feet on their shoulders they will find some of what I've given to them to be valuable, and to help them be strong.

I thought about love: and must acknowledge once again that the myth that is romance, mystery and magic is what feeds my soul. In their absence I bury my heart deeply and fill the empty space with the mundane trivia we all call "living". For some, that is enough. For me, it is a quiet sadness that does not go away. When there is that vacuum, it is a painful empty place and I seal it off and scar it over.

I thought about spirituality: and once again renewed the awe I always feel in the mountains. I realized whatever the essence of God really is, it manifests itself to each of us in unique and powerful ways—not through the pompous rituals of men or careful studies of literary liturgy—but in a tiny purple wildflower or the smokey-blue color of someone's eyes or the call of an eagle in flight, or the touch of a child's hand. In those ways, I have known the God I believe in, and still refuse to confine that higher power to a box labeled under a particular brand-name "religion".

The Dragon taught me some things. Perhaps I already knew them, perhaps not, but all the same they are new things now. Learning about your "self" can be a difficult lesson—very humbling, most enlightening, pretty scary—difficult to share with anyone but the mirror on your most self-confident days. But if you assimilate it, use it, and grow from it, the lesson is worthwhile. Not an easy assignment, I assure you.

I learned that I am able to discard what I don't value if I want to—but it takes a concerted effort. My life has been full of things that in the end are chaff and will be discarded. Hiding in the chaff, though, are grains and kernels of great value and the secret is to know the difference.

I learned that my own spirituality is deep and solid, and bigger than the God I learned about in Protestant Sunday School classes as a child. Someone once said that religion is for those who fear hell—and spirituality is for those who have been there. Well, yes. The God of my universe understands that distinction, even if it's merely a concept in the mind of man—which makes it all the more powerful whenever I've stumbled accidentally on the threshold of tasting my own mortality.

I learned I do not enjoy my own counsel when it gets too close to the truth of things—it is too painful—but when I listen to it I trust it. It takes concerted effort for me to settle down and listen to the small voice of reason in my mind. I am good at debate, and quick to point out flaws in my own reasoning. But the value in my intelligence is only found when I listen to it and then use it.

I learned the love I have is deep and intense, and those who have some of it don't realize what it costs me. Even though it is given without the expectation that it will be returned, sometimes I've unconsciously made it conditional and lost the power of it because of the details. Only love freely given will ever become a circle—and I need to believe in circles.

I learned that confining this wild streak is not possible, even though living with it has always been (and always will be) my curse as well as my blessing. I fear it is there to stay, and if channeled, creates an interesting composite. Those around me must find it tedious and to them I apologize. But when I face it squarely I accept and acknowledge that it's part of who I am. For then the compromise becomes a gift.

There are things in life that just happen—some you choose, some you don't. But every once in a while, if you listen very carefully and approach very respectfully, you can hear a Dragon speak softly to your soul. My life has been changed by this most auspicious Journey on the Back of a Dragon. I hope you find your own auspicious journey.

Tashi Delek!

Druk's Path looking across the Dragon's Back Ridge
Location: Between Paro and Thimphu, Bhutan

Druk - watchful guardian of his Bhutan mountain top

Beverly Lynne Gray's books

Druk's Path
(the original journal, winner of
San Diego Unpublished Manuscripts Award)

Thunderstorms and Rainbows
(winner of San Diego Book Award for poetry)

You can order these books by contacting

BLACK FOREST PRESS
P.O. Box 6342
Chula Vista, CA 91909-6342
1-800-451-9404

You may also order from the shopping cart
on the Web site at
www.blackforestpress.com

About the Author

BEVERLY LYNNE GRAY was raised in Arizona surrounded by a large family and a variety of pets. Currently residing in southern California, she continues to write and balances her life with career, community service, outdoor activities, family, and friends. She collects dragons, rides horses, and wears hats—the rest is subject to change without much notice.